THE
MACRAMÉ
BIBLE

ROBYN GOUGH

The complete reference guide to
macramé knots, patterns, motifs & more

DAVID & CHARLES

www.davidandcharles.com

CONTENTS

NET PATTERNS

FOUR-CORD CHAINS

SIX-CORD CHAINS

PROJECT IDEAS

INTRODUCTION

Thank you for choosing to pick up this book. If it's your first time delving into the world of macramé then I'm thrilled to say welcome, but even if you've done macramé before, or consider yourself a pro, there is plenty in this book for you. This keep-it-on-the-shelf manual covers all things macramé and is designed to get you started with this ancient pastime and to help you to go on to develop a creative practice of your own. Filled with step-by-step instructions, practical hints and tips, and all the fine details for making projects, even if you are an experienced macramé crafter there are lessons and processes here for you, too.

ABOUT ME

When I'm not making things with my hands, I'm daydreaming about making things instead. Escaping life's everyday tasks, I enjoy imagining trying out projects, visualizing tying motions, or designing shapes and combining patterns together in my mind. I've always taken comfort from thinking in this way, and I've had some of my best ideas when driving to the supermarket! This book is right for you if, like me, you enjoy focusing on making, have a curiosity to understand how macramé art is made, and a hope to design beautiful things yourself.

When did my own obsession with macramé begin? As a ten-year-old, I first discovered knotting when practising the 'art' of creative shoelace tying for customized roller skates and trainers. As a teenager, I explored further by braiding and knotting my hair, which created some interesting looks, much to my family's surprise. But it was as a student at university, wanting to put my own stamp on my first-ever rented property, that I really began to explore macramé, initially decorating with plant hangers and smaller macramé motifs, then gaining confidence to make larger wall hangings and tapestries. Now, nearly a decade later, I have macramé to thank for so many things! My pastime and hobby has transformed into an online craft business that has allowed me to reach so many people across the globe through the power of the internet, social media and in-person workshops too.

I know from my own experiences that learning the craft of macramé can take you on a fulfilling and creative journey of self-expression. This book will give you the building blocks to discover where the magic of macramé will take you.

HOW TO USE THIS BOOK

Macramé, or the art of knotting, is thousands of years old and it has survived so long, no doubt, because it is not only beautiful but practical too. The aim of this book is to provide you with an essential resource of all the techniques, but also to encourage you to develop designs of your own as your skills progress.

We start by introducing the tools and materials you will need as well as a few essential skills. There are tips on getting started and finishing methods, too, as well as useful troubleshooting advice.

Then technique chapters build to provide you with a comprehensive directory to this fascinating craft. Knotting chapters offer an extensive resource for knot families, from single-strand knots to half hitch knots, as well as standalone decorative knots, all explained in a simple and easy to understand way with illustrated step-by-step instruction for the tying methods that you'll be sure to return to again and again.

In the net patterns, four-cord chains and six-cord chains chapters, you'll discover small practice pieces showing you how to combine knots to create simple shapes, which is the first step to following macramé patterns and creating macramé designs of your own. These provide you with the opportunity to practise tying essential macramé knots, mastering making knots that face in all directions, mirroring actions and giving you a muscle memory, all without taking too much time or using too much material.

The final chapter, Project Ideas, offers a wonderful range of patterns for you to explore your developing macramé skills. Each is graded so that you can see at a glance if the project is right for your skill level (see Project Ratings). Also, the knots required to make each project are helpfully listed so that you can brush up on your tying technique before making a start on your selected design. You can choose your project knowing that all the techniques required are included in the techniques chapters for you to refer back to. And, as your confidence and tying skills grow, I encourage you to personalize your designs and express your style.

PROJECT RATINGS

Easy Beginners

Easy to Intermediate

Intermediate to Advanced

Advanced and Beyond

TOOLS AND MATERIALS

Apart from macramé cord itself, there are very few tools and materials manufactured specifically for the craft of macramé. I've found that part of the fun has been repurposing items around the home. That being said, there are some essentials as well as commonly used items that can be revolutionary to an enthusiastic maker, as outlined in this section.

MACRAMÉ CORD

The most common question I'm asked when teaching macramé is, 'What material should I use to knot with?' The simple answer is, whatever you are most comfortable with, but my recommendation, based not least on its ready availability, is cotton cord (or string or rope as it may sometimes be called).

TYPES OF COTTON MACRAMÉ CORD

Cotton is the hero fibre of this craft for so many reasons: it's strong; it dyes well, so can be found in many vibrant colours; and, as it is often created as a by-product of the textiles industry, it is often manufactured in an ecological way. Let's look at your options:

3-ply macramé cord (or rope): This is composed of three strands twisted together to form a uniform rope. It has a traditional appearance and is a go-to for achieving that classic macramé look. It holds its shape well and has a low tangle tendency when worked through the hands, making it perfect for beginners. If unravelled, it produces a wavy 'mermaid' fringe.

Single-ply macramé cord (or string): This is made of many fine base strings twisted together once for a smoother finish. It has a more contemporary feel and is available in a wide variety of colours and is a popular choice with modern macramé artists. This cord combs out easily for super-smooth and show-stopping block fringes, but it tangles a little more easily than 3-ply so might be better suited for intermediate makers with some experience.

Braided cord (or rope): A specialist cord that is less readily available than either 3-ply or single-ply cord. It's expensive and as its braided composition makes it time consuming when combing out into a fringe, I would not recommend its use if the project has a fringe element.

All types of cotton cord, whichever you choose, are strong enough to hold incredibly heavy weights, such as plant pots for example. However, cotton cord is not weatherproof, so if making outdoor projects, a garden jute would be a better choice! I have seen macramé made from jersey and wool yarn, but I do not recommend using stretchy materials such as these as it's very difficult to produce regular sized knots and to pull them tightly enough to be secure.

It's a good idea to build up a stash of different cotton cord thicknesses suitable for making a range of different projects (see What Macramé Cord Thickness Should I Buy?), but it's important to store them correctly, on a good, strong shelf in a dry, clean environment. If you want to keep your cord soft and fluffy, never store it in a damp or dusty environment, such as a garage.

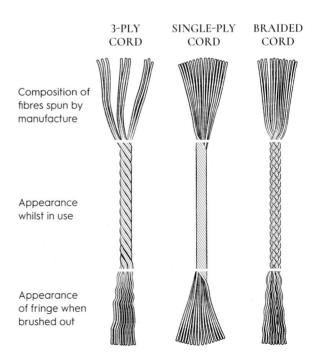

| | 3-PLY CORD | SINGLE-PLY CORD | BRAIDED CORD |

Composition of fibres spun by manufacture

Appearance whilst in use

Appearance of fringe when brushed out

WHAT MACRAMÉ CORD THICKNESS SHOULD I BUY?

Although technically any cord will make any project, I have based my recommendations on my own preferences. For more advice on working with macramé cord, see Getting Started.

Project	2mm (3⁄32in)	3mm (1⁄8in)	4mm (5⁄32in)	5mm (3⁄16in)	6mm (1⁄4in)
Jewellery	Yes	Yes	N/R	N/R	N/R
Mini wall hanging	N/R	Yes	Yes	N/R	N/R
Feather or leaf	N/R	Yes	Yes	Yes	N/R
Small wall hanging	N/R	Yes	Yes	Yes	N/R
Plant hanger	N/R	Yes	Yes	Yes	N/R
Medium wall hanging	N/R	Yes	Yes	Yes	Yes
Table runner	N/R	Yes	Yes	Yes	N/R
Large wall hanging	N/R	N/R	Yes	Yes	Yes
Extra-large (XL) hanging	N/R	N/R	N/R	Yes	Yes
Wedding arch	N/R	N/R	N/R	Yes	Yes

N/R = Not recommended

Note: cord sizes listed as N/R are only advisory; however, remember that choosing a cord that is small for a larger project could be very time consuming, while choosing a cord that is too large for smaller projects can take away detail. The finished sizes given for the projects included in this book are based on the cord thicknesses listed in the Materials list, and sizes will vary if you use a different cord weight than that demonstrated.

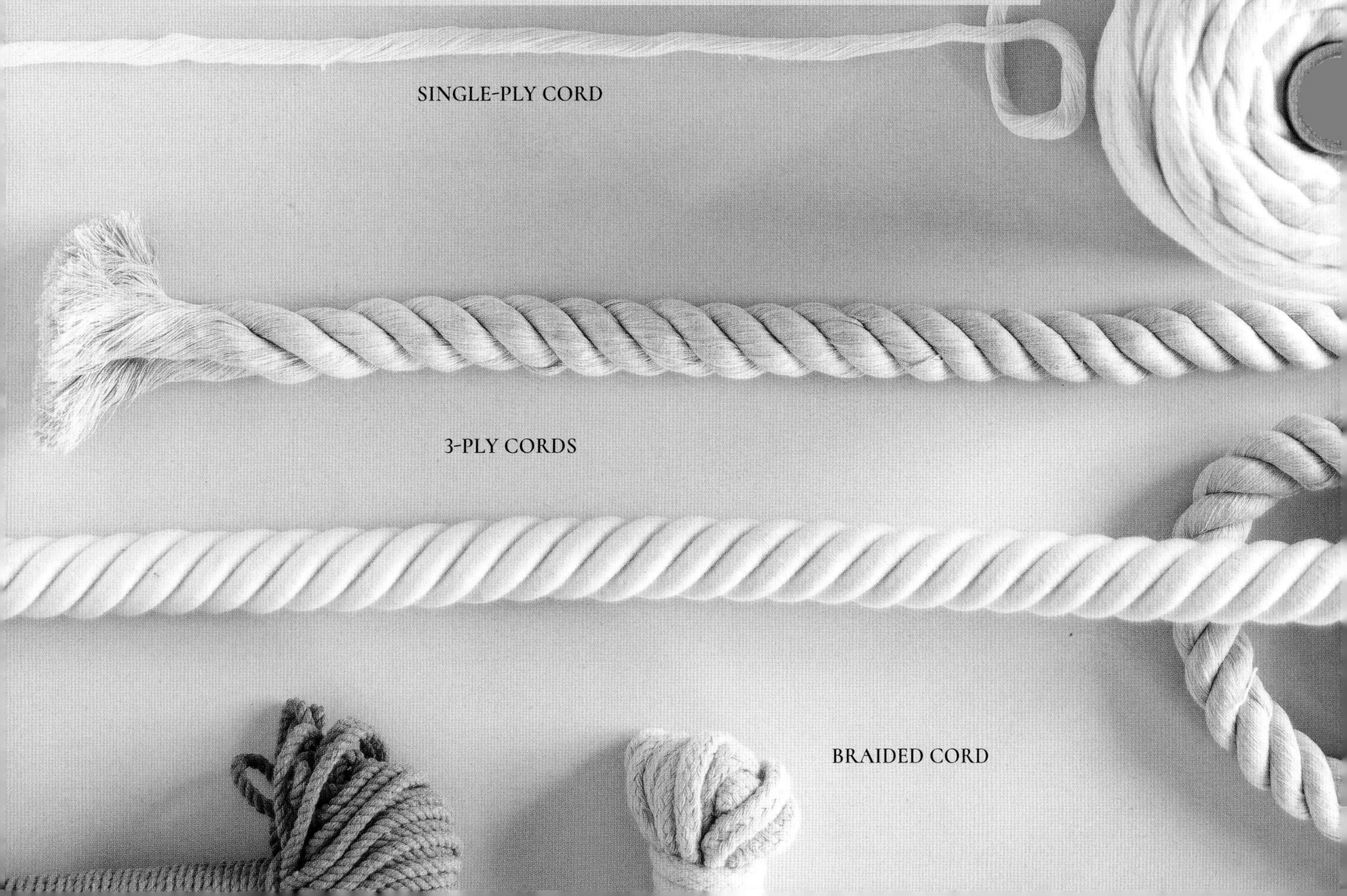

SINGLE-PLY CORD

3-PLY CORDS

BRAIDED CORD

USEFUL ITEMS

Tools can be a game changer when learning a new craft or when working on a specific type of project. Here is a list of recommended items and their uses.

TOOLS AND SUNDRIES

Clothes rail and S-hooks: Clothes rails are great for hanging up long projects, such as wall hangings or plant hangers, for ease of working; if buying new, choose one where the main rail can be adjusted, to be raised or lowered, as you work. S-hooks are available from hardware stores and online and will help you to secure your foundation item onto the rail.

Macramé board (designed by Anne Dilker for the Beadsmith) or cork board, with push pins or T-pins: A macramé board (or cork board) is a brilliant item to have for working on smaller projects on a table top.

Saw: For cutting wooden dowels to size; make sure the blade is sharp, and keep fingers well clear.

Dressmaker's scissors: Keep them nice and sharp for cutting fringes and lots of cords at once. Watch your fingers and if you have long hair, make sure it is tied back!

Rotary cutter: Ideal for accurate trimming of unravelled fringes on smaller projects.

Needle and thread; crochet hook: For tucking away ends and tidying up project backs.

Glue gun: For ensuring knots are secured in place for hard-working, functional projects like the keyring accessories.

Pet hairbrush: For untangling single-ply cord for show-stopping fringes

Beads: For adding stylish accents to projects; search for wooden beads with larger holes when shopping online.

Fabric glue or fabric stiffener: For preserving the shape of macramé feathers and leaves (I use Modge Podge Stiffy).

Clear tape or masking tape: Useful for fastening cords to a work surface and for managing cords when working.

FOUNDATIONS FOR MACRAMÉ

Dowels: When making macramé wall hangings, it is likely that you will mount your cords onto a length of wooden dowel, although a found stick makes an attractive alternative. Dowel lengths are readily available from hardware stores.

Rings: These are another good foundation for mounting hanging cords onto: metal rings are better than wooden rings for plant hanger starters as they are stronger, but wooden rings are great for smaller projects like the Christmas decorations.

Keyrings clasps and findings: Specific to wristlet projects or handbag charms and keyring accessories, there are plenty of styles available online and in craft stores.

KEYRING CLASPS

S-HOOKS

METAL HOOPS AND RINGS

WOODEN DOWELS
OR STICKS

CROCHET
HOOK

WOODEN BEADS

SCISSORS

WOODEN
RINGS

ROTARY CUTTER

DRESSMAKER'S
SCISSORS

ESSENTIAL SKILLS

Once you've chosen your cord and gathered your tools, you're ready to get started. Well almost. There are just a few helpful tips that I need to share to ensure your success, including setting up a working environment appropriate to your chosen project, and how to cut and manage cord.

PROJECT SET-UP

FOR SMALLER PROJECTS

Smaller projects, such as the knotting practice pieces, keyrings and Christmas decorations featured in this book, can be made whilst sitting down at your desk or a table. It can be helpful when tying knots in this way to have the ability to fix cords to your work surface. I find that masking tapes, particularly those that are 'high tack' such as painter's tapes, can be a useful and low cost tool.

Although not essential, another item you might find useful, especially if you are a first-time knotter, is a 'macramé board'. This is a foam rectangle that has long slits cut into its scalloped edges into which you can slide your cords so that they are held in place securely as you tie your knots, although they are easy enough to remove again once you have finished. T-pins or push pins can be used to hold knots in place once tied and a grid printed onto the board is a useful reference for making consistently spaced knots. Macramé boards are widely available online and in craft stores, but a cork board works too when practising knots.

FOR MEDIUM TO LARGE PROJECTS AND WALL HANGINGS

Clothes rails act as a 'one item to fit many situations' tool for macramé makers and I strongly recommend them. Any macramé project that when finished is hung vertically, benefits from being created whilst being hung vertically, too. A clothes rail that has adjustable height features allows makers to stand and sit whilst tying their knots, and I find that cheaper versions are often the most effective. They tend to have plastic side screws making them very lightweight and easy to move, especially if they have wheels, and when not being used for making, they can provide an easy-to-put-away tool station for storing cords and equipment.

An S-hook, or pair of S-hooks, is recommended when using a clothes rail for making, so that you can hang your project up easily and flip it around to complete any finishing touches. The Pattern Notes provided for the projects in the Projects Ideas section include advice on when to use a clothes rail and ways it can help you in certain situations.

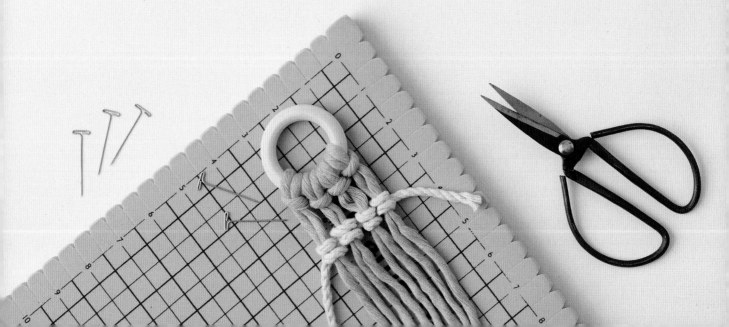

TERMINOLOGY

Before getting hands on, familiarize yourself with some of the terminology used throughout this book.

Cord: I have used this term to refer to any material used to make the macramé, whatever it may be.

Knot: A general term meaning to tie or fasten one or more cords.

Working cord: The length of cord being manipulated and moved to tie the knot.

Worked / committed cord: A cord that is committed to a knot or knots.

Unworked / hanging cords: Cords that are not yet used in knots but have been prepared, attached and are ready for knotting.

Static cord: The length of cord not being moved, often having the working cord tied onto or around it.

Foundation: An item used in a project for macramé to be created onto. This can be a dowel, a length of cord, a metal or wooden ring, or a keyring finding.

Wrap / loop: Where the working cord is looped around one or more static cords.

Weave: To use a working cord to go over and under or around static cords.

Bundle: To hold or group together cords with one hand.

Fringe / fringe line: Cord lengths that hang for a final finish; often just attached with lark's head knots and that are unworked.

Sinnet: A column of the same knot tied repetitively.

Row: Used to describe the order to work in, either left to right or right to left; not a physical row but an imaginary line that keeps all knots placed together.

Layers: Cords or knots that fall over or under another collection of cords or knots, often seen on talisman wall hangings.

Picot: A loop of cord created to be a decorative feature within a project or sinnet of knots.

Chain: A term for a collection of knots tied into shapes repeated vertically; often seen on talisman wall hangings.

HOW TO CUT AND MANAGE CORDS

In the Materials list for each of the projects in this book, I have given the overall length of cord required in the thickness used for the sample as made. To achieve similar results, it's advisable to keep within 1–2mm of the recommended cord. To cut the overall length, place the reel of macramé cord on the floor between your feet; standing above it, find the beginning of the cord, pinch it between your finger and thumb and lift it vertically, allowing the cord to unravel in a circular motion ready to measure and cut.

The Preparation list for each project identifies the lengths of cord to be cut from your overall cord length. Whether you cut these as-you-go, or whether you cut them to the lengths required before you start, this is a matter of personal preference. These are generally cut generously so that fringes can be cut to your taste, but mainly because having a bit of extra length makes it easier to tie knots in the right place.

When buying and cutting cord, use either the metric or the imperial measurements given – do not switch between the two.

RULE OF THUMB FOR CUTTING CORD LENGTHS

When you get to designing your own projects, how do you know what cord lengths to measure and cut? A rule of thumb often cited is 4.5 x the planned-for finished length of your project, plus an extra amount to account for the fringe length once cut.

While the rule of thumb is a good starting place, there are situations where you will need to allow for more as some knots require more cord to tie than others. Half hitch knots, for example, and diagonal half hitches in particular, gobble up cotton and in this instance 6.5 x the finished length of the hanging is sensible!

Ultimately, precise planning of a project is desirable to minimize leftover cord at the end, but if you're making something new and original, a certain amount of waste is inevitable. One practical step you can take is to try to locate a pattern of a similar project that uses similar knots in a similar quantity as your starting point, then add on to the cord lengths they suggest for safe measure. Remember, you can always keep your offcuts in a bag and use them to make smaller items like leaves and feathers (see Project Ideas).

HOW TO BUNDLE LENGTHS

When working on larger wall hangings with very long lengths of cord, it can be useful to bundle or wrap up the lengths of each hanging cord to save time. This can be done using the following method:

1. Take a long single length of cord. Working approximately 60cm (24in) down, wrap the remaining length of cord around the fingers of one hand (A). Leave a tail of unwrapped cord of about 50cm (20in).

2. Pull the wrapped cord off the hand and pinch it in the middle using the index finger and thumb (B).

3. Take the remaining tail and wrap it around the centre of the cords where it was pinched. Leave 10cm (4in) of cord unwrapped (C).

4. Place the remaining length of cord through the space between the bottom of the central wraps and the bottom loops of cord (D). Do not pull this tight, simply weave it through and allow it to rest. The cord is now loosely bundled and can be unwrapped and adjusted when knotting.

GETTING STARTED

Although all macramé projects have knots in common, some macramé projects benefit from taking initial steps that help form their signature looks, or functions. Any maker embarking on these projects for the first time will benefit from the following suggestions and techniques.

PRACTISING KNOTS

Except where advised differently, all of the knots and their step-by-step instructions featured in the knotting reference chapters of this book can be made by sitting and working at a desk or table. When practising making knots for the first time, some cord, some scissors and some masking tape are really all you need, although a cork board and some pins can be helpful, too (see Essential Skills: Project Set-Up).

PRACTISING SINNETS

Many of the knotting reference chapters feature sinnets of knots, which are a great way to practise essential knots as you'll be continuously repeating the knot-tying steps to form a column of the same knot. They require multiple cords to make and these cords are fastened together with an overhand knot.

HOW TO START A SINNET WITH MULTIPLE CORDS

1. Taking your lengths of pre-cut cord, rest them vertically and pass the ends of the cords over themselves to form a loop (A).

2. Pass the ends through the loop (B) and pull them downwards to form the knot (C), paying attention to the placement of the finished knot as it's best to have it close to the top of the cord ends to give you the length you'll need to complete the sinnet.

A

B

C

STARTING SMALL PROJECTS

The smaller practice pieces and projects featured in this book often require a foundation item for working onto. The keyrings, for example, require a keyring finding or a fastening clasp, and the Christmas decorations need wooden rings. Each project specifies the item or way of working, but what they all have in common is that there is no need to work vertically when making smaller items.

STARTING PLANT HANGERS

Classic macramé plant hangers have a shape that makes them unique as a project, although without a plant pot in place they really just look like a long collection of knots! All macramé plant hangers start with a way to hang them up so that they can support the weight of the plant and its pot. Plant hangers when completed are very long and thin, so it's sensible to tie the knots when making them whilst standing up, using a clothes rail and S-hooks to help you. The plant hangers in the Project Ideas section use the Wrap Knot Hanging Loop technique to make a strong corded loop at the top of the plant hanger that can be personalized with colour additions, too, and the steps for mastering this Getting Started skill are featured in Single-Strand Knots. However, some makers start plant hangers with the addition of a metal ring or small metal hoop. It is important however to avoid using wooden rings for this as they can crack under the weight of the plant and its pot.

HOW TO START A PLANT HANGER ON A METAL HOOP

If you decide to use a metal hoop, you'll need to attach your cords to it using a forward facing lark's head knot (see Single-Strand Knots).

1. Measure and cut all cord lengths required according to the pattern instructions.

2. Place your metal ring onto a S-hook suspended from a clothes rails.

3. Hold all the cut cords together vertically and fold them at the mid point to create a loop shape.

4. Place the loop through the metal ring, keeping hold of the loop shape with your hand (A).

5. Take the tail lengths of the cords through the loop shape (B).

6. Pull the tail lengths to form a forward facing lark's head knot to secure the cords to the ring (C), which will look like (D) on the reverse.

STARTING WALL HANGINGS

All wall hanging projects are hung onto a wall so will benefit from being made whilst hanging vertically on a clothes rail. It is very common for wall hangings to be made onto a wooden dowel or onto a branch or stick. Dowels are smooth and uniform in shape and branches or sticks are sourced from nature and have various forms and thicknesses.

To attach cord onto a dowel, lark's head knots are used. This could be either the forward or the reverse lark's head knot as described in Single-Strand Knots.

Some wall hangings do not have a dowel foundation, and instead are made onto a foundation cord, as seen in the bunting garland for example (see Project Ideas), although once again forward or reverse lark's head knots are used to attach the working cords.

LOOPING LARK'S HEAD TECHNIQUE

Most wall hangings normally begin by measuring and cutting cord lengths, folding them in half and attaching them at the fold point to a dowel, stick or foundation cord using lark's head knots. However, when projects have a curved top feature rather than a straight line, as seen in the angel wings, or when a fringing line needs to be added, for the triple layer talisman for example, the looping lark's head technique needs to be used.

This technique enables you to create a long curved cord line underneath a dowel, onto which working cords can be attached rather than adding them directly onto the dowel, as follows:

1. Measure and cut a long length of cord as instructed in the project instructions. Attach it towards the left-hand end of the dowel using a lark's head knot, so that the hanging cord is shorter on the left-hand side and longer on the right-hand side.

2. Take the (longer) right-hand cord and move it along the dowel to the desired distance, making a length of cord that forms a U-shape curve (A).

3. Working the tail of the cord, tie another lark's head knot using the following method: take the length over the dowel resting behind it; pull the end over itself and to the right-hand side creating a loop over the dowel (B); create a second loop by pulling the length under the dowel and back over the top, placing it next to the first loop and taking it under itself to form a pretzel shape (C).

4. Pull the cords to manipulate and fasten the second lark's head knot to complete the curved line (D).

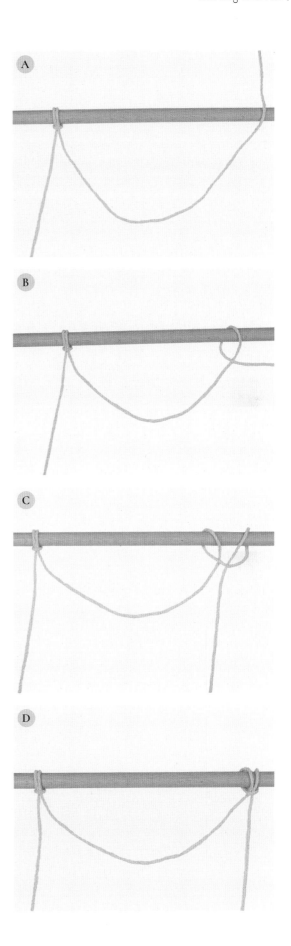

FINISHING METHODS

Once the knotting is complete, there is usually very little that needs to be done before you can enjoy your macramé masterpieces – a little tidying up maybe, making a hanging cord to display a wall hanging and, perhaps most fun of all, some creative fringing if you choose.

CREATING A HANGING LOOP

The simplest way to hang a wall hanging for display is with a single or double picture hook, and for this a hanging loop is required. I like to create these after I have finished the wall hanging so I can assess how long or wide the cords need to reach, as follows:

1. Measure and cut two lengths of cord to place either side of the finished piece. These should be the same length, but the length itself is project dependent.

2. Place the cords onto the dowel either side of the project using a lark's head knot of your choice (either the same as the rest of the hanging cords or the opposite for contrast).

3. Join the ends of the cords with an overhand knot. Tighten the knot to ensure it's in the middle to help the hanging hang straight on its hooks (A). Trim the cord ends as you prefer.

TIDYING UP THE BACK

Although not strictly necessary, it can be nice if you are gifting a piece you have made, or if you are selling an item, to pay some attention to the reverse of the piece, taking steps to tidy it up if appropriate so it looks organized.

For example, for pixel-style wall hangings like the leopard print wall hanging (see Project Ideas) made using vertical double half hitch knots, where the cords that make the design are carried over the back, I recommend either cutting and trimming the loops – this is safe to do on this style of hanging as the knots are secure – or simply covering the reverse with self-adhesive felt in an appropriate colour. While this works for this style of wall hanging, where the knots are so tightly formed together that there is no way to see through it, it is not recommended for most macramé wall hangings as they have a see-through element to them.

CUTTING FRINGES

Cutting fringes can be make or break for a wall hanging project, so it's important to do it in stages if you are not confident of the length that will look best. And remember to consider the fringe shape, too. Not all projects need to have a straight fringe; sometimes it can be effective to have a curved bottom, a pointed bottom or even an inverted triangle bottom, like a pennant.

Before cutting a fringe, I recommend that you leave your finished wall hanging suspended from your clothes rail for a day or two after knotting, to let gravity give you an idea of how the fringe cords will rest when not being tied and moved around.

When you are ready to begin, first ensure your clothes rail is level by using a spirit level. Make sure your dowel is suspended from matching S-hooks and check that the dowel is level also, again using a spirit level.

Start trimming, cutting small amounts off at a time, starting first with the longest you want the fringe to be. Step back and take a look to see if you are happy. Selecting the outside cords, run both hands down them at the same pace until you get to the end to check that they are the same lengths, and use a dressmaker's tape to spot check cord lengths, trimming small amounts to correct if necessary.

CREATIVE FRINGING TIPS

- For projects made using single-ply cord, fringes can be easily brushed out using a pet hairbrush (sometimes called a slicker brush).

- For extra smooth single-ply fringes, use a clothes steamer, or even hair straighteners, to smooth fibres to be completely straight.

- For projects made using 3-ply cord, fringes can be made wavy by going through the individual hanging cords and separating the plies apart. This is best done by starting at the ends of the cords and working upwards to unravel.

- One way to finish a fringe is with a single overhand knot tied at the very bottom of each fringe cord.

- Or you could add in some tassels, either at random intervals as seen in the tassels chain, or on all fringe cords as seen on the triple layer talisman (see Project Ideas).

- Or you could create a fringe that has a few eye-catching decorative knots, such as the leaf knot for example, placed at random intervals throughout (see Decorative Knots).

- The fringe lengths provide you with another opportunity to create a knotting pattern, as can be seen in the fishtail chains talisman where an alternating square knot pattern has been created within the top fringe layer (see Project Ideas).

- It can be very effective to choose a knot from the family of knots featured in the main body of the wall hanging and to experiment with placing them within its fringes.

TROUBLESHOOTING

Even when considering all of the tips and tricks included for projects, sometimes problems do arise despite good planning. Included here are some ways of overcoming obstacles and tricky situations so that should you have a problem, particularly when designing your own patterns, you can work your way around them.

RUN OUT OF CORD

When working on wall hanging projects, particularly if you are not following a predetermined pattern, it can become apparent that a cord within your working cords is coming up shorter than the others. Depending on the knots being used, it can be possible to address single short cord problems, if detected early.

OPTION 1 - SWAPPING THE CORD

When noticing that a single cord is shorter than the rest of your working cords, do not wait until you reach the very end of the cord to act. If there is a cord that is much shorter than the others, it's possible to abandon it behind the project, introducing a new longer length in its place, as follows:

1. Identify the cord that is shorter than all the others and prepare to swap it out for one that is the correct length (A).

2. Measure a single length of cord that is the same length as the surrounding cords, add on an extra 50cm (20in) to this length and cut. Take a clip and attach the tail of the new length to the clothes rail or the project dowel to hold it place. Take the short cord and some masking tape and tape it out of the way on the back of the project so that you no longer include it in the working cords (B).

3. Continue with your project pattern, using the new length of cord to tie your knots (C).

4. At the end of the project pattern, remove the clip that was holding the length end in place and trim the excess cord at the back of the project. It can be useful to stitch the ends to the back of a knot to avoid fraying. Remove the masking tape from the short cord and trim the excess, again stitching if you wish.

A

B

C

OPTION 2 – WEAVING INTO A SINNET OF SQUARE KNOTS

In the case where the static cords are too short within a sinnet of square knots (D), new cord can be introduced with the following process:

1. Measure a length of cord and fold it in half. Place it on top of the static cords (E).

2. Tie the square knot around all the static cords (F). The shorter cords behind will eventually run out but cannot be seen as the new cords will be over the top (G).

MISS A KNOT OR MISS A CORD

Macramé projects are tied from top to bottom and all of your cords and knots for a project should be used to weave in with the ones that came before. On occasion you may look back on some knots and realize that you have missed a knot or missed out a cord.

Unfortunately, the only way to correct a missed knot is to untie the knots below it or around it. It may be, however, that the untrained eye may not notice that a mistake has been made, and I'd encourage you to carry on with your project as if this hasn't happened. All handicrafts have a handmade finish to them, and sometimes this means they are not 'perfect'.

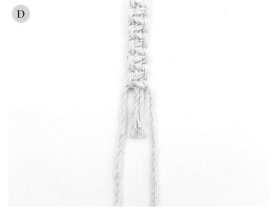

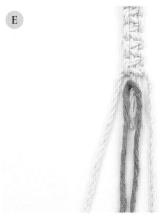

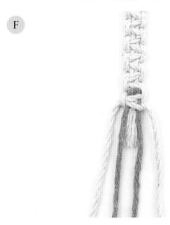

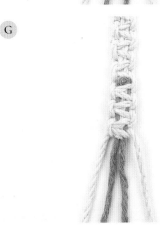

SINGLE-STRAND KNOTS

Single-strand knots require only one length of cord to be manipulated in their formation. Pay close attention to the tying movements, however, as the looping actions and the weaving of a single end in different directions creates the distinctive look that differentiates one from another. Also included here are lark's head knots, the cast-on classic used to begin most macramé projects, as well as the wrap knot hanging loop, which is a great way to start that most popular of macramé pieces, the plant hanger.

OVERHAND KNOT

The overhand knot is one of the most commonly used functional knots in everyday life. In macramé it's often used to secure ends or to tie multiple hanging cords together. It is shown here being tied on a single cord, and it is sometimes taught by the ends passing over a closed hand, hence its name.

1. With a single strand of cord held in place vertically, take the cord end and pass it over itself to form a loop (A).

2. Take the cord end through the loop and back down, then pull the cord in opposite directions to form the knot (B, C, D).

 A

 B

C

D

FIGURE OF EIGHT KNOT

Similar to the overhand knot, the figure of eight knot is a more decorative securing knot, often used to finish hanging cords to prevent fraying. Its name describes the path the cord end takes to travel over and under itself to shape and form the knot's structure.

1. With a single strand of cord held in place vertically, take the cord end and pass it over itself to form a loop (A).

2. Bring the right-hand end of the cord under the left-hand end to form the top loop (B) and continue to weave the cord end over and under the bottom loop (C).

3. Pull the cord ends in opposite directions to form the knot (D).

A
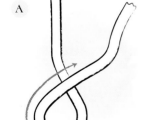

B
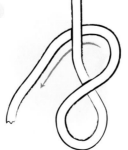

C

D

BARREL KNOT

The barrel knot is a secure decorative knot that can add texture and visual interest to fringing, creating pleasing eye-catching accents.

1. With a single strand of cord held in place vertically, take the cord end and pass it over itself to form a loop. Holding the loop in place by pinching it between your index finger and thumb, take the cord end up through the loop and wrap the length around the loop, returning it to the front (A, B).

2. Continue to wrap the cord around the loop to complete four wraps in total, bringing the cord end over the bottom part of the loop after the final wrap (C, D).

3. Gently pull on the working end of the cord only; the wrapped loops will take on a twisted round form (E).

4. Pull tightly at the end to achieve the final knot (F).

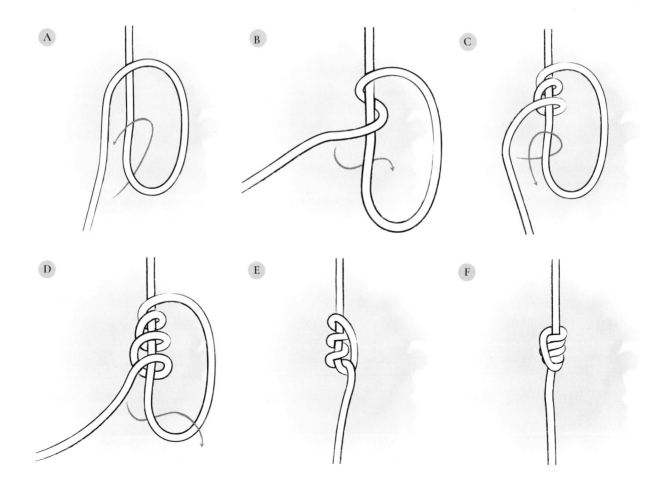

FORWARD LARK'S HEAD KNOT

The forward lark's head knot is used to fasten cords onto a foundation cord or dowel when beginning a macramé project, and most wall hangings start this way. It is usually tied with the ends of the cord even, as demonstrated.

1. Fold your length of cord in half so that the ends meet, making a loop in the middle. Take the loop and place it over the dowel so the loop is at the back (A).

2. Place the cord ends through the loop (B).

3. Pull the cord ends down to secure the knot. On a forward lark's head knot the loop creates a line beneath the dowel (C).

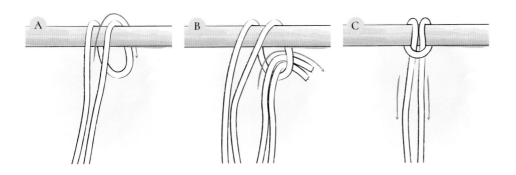

REVERSE LARK'S HEAD KNOT

The reverse lark's head knot is tied from behind the dowel working towards the front, so that the loop line is hidden at the back of the knot

1. Fold your length of cord in half so that the ends meet, making a loop in the middle. Take the loop and place it over the dowel so the loop is at the front (A).

2. Place the cord ends through the loop (B).

3. Pull the cord ends down to secure the knot. With a reverse lark's head knot, no loop line is visible beneath the dowel (C).

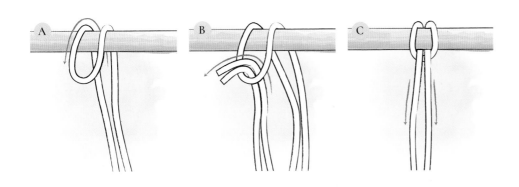

VERTICAL LARK'S HEAD KNOT (RIGHT FACING)

The vertical lark's head knot, demonstrated here as a fastening method for two individual hanging cords, is often seen in macramé projects. There is a static cord and a working cord. For the right facing vertical lark's head knot, the right-hand working cord is moved to create the knot onto the left-hand static cord.

1. Place the working cord at a right angle over the static cord (A).

2. Weave the working cord under the static cord and rest it on top of itself to create the first loop (B).

3. Pass the working cord under the static cord (C), bringing it back over the static cord and under itself to create a second loop (D).

4. Pull the ends of the working cord gently in opposite directions to form the pretzel-shaped knot (E, F).

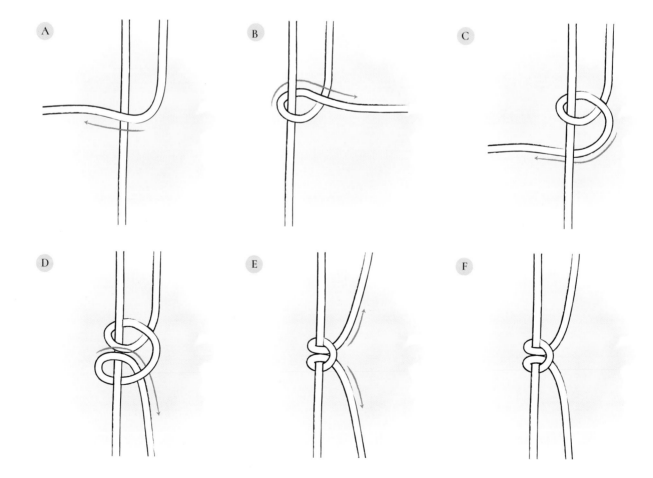

VERTICAL LARK'S HEAD KNOT (LEFT FACING)

For the left facing vertical lark's head knot, the left-hand working cord is moved to create the knot onto the right-hand static cord. The left facing vertical lark's head knot (in grey) is shown continuing on the same static cord as the right facing vertical lark's head knot, to illustrate the mirroring of the actions.

1. Place the working cord at a right angle over the static cord. Weave the working cord under the static cord and rest it on top of itself to create the first loop (A).

2. Pass the working cord under the static cord, bringing it back over the static cord and under itself to create a second loop (B).

3. Pull the ends of the working cord gently in opposite directions to form the pretzel-shaped knot (C).

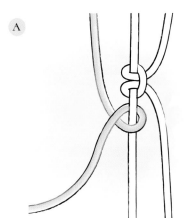

A

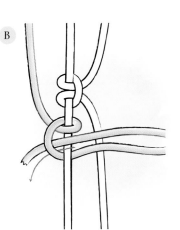

B

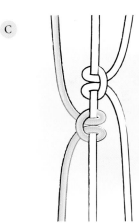

C

ALTERNATING LARK'S HEAD SINNET

This is the perfect practice piece to develop the muscle memory needed to tie vertical lark's head knots in both directions. By alternating right and left facing lark's head knots you will get used to mirroring the actions. The knots are tied in the same way, just facing in opposite directions. It sounds simple, but in practice mirroring actions can feel unnatural to begin with.

1. Cut three cord lengths: 1 x 50cm (20in) of white for the central static cord; 1 x 120cm (47in) of grey for the left-hand working cord; and 1 x 120cm (47in) of mustard for the right-hand working cord. Aligning the cords at one end, tie them together with an overhand knot (A).

2. Take the right-hand working (mustard) cord and tie a right facing vertical lark's head knot over the static (white) cord, referring to Vertical Lark's Head Knot (Right Facing) (B).

3. Take the left-hand working (grey) cord and tie a left facing vertical lark's head knot over the static (white) cord, referring to Vertical Lark's Head Knot (Left Facing), securing it directly beneath the knot above (C).

4. Continue tying vertical lark's head knots, alternating between the right facing technique for the mustard cord and the left facing technique for the grey cord, until you reach the end of the cords (D).

5. To finish, tie the ends with an overhand knot to secure (E).

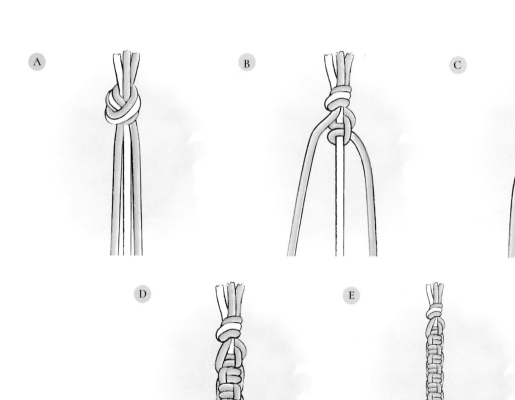

LARK'S HEAD PICOT SINNET

This variation on the alternating lark's head sinnet sees the addition of decorative loops, a great way to add texture and interest. It's incredibly simple to do when you know how to tie the knots, so first master the left and right facing vertical lark's head knots, then give it a try.

1. Cut three lengths of cord: 1 x 50cm (20in) length of white cord for the central static cord; 1 x 120cm (47in) length of grey cord for the left-hand working cord; and 1 x 120cm (47in) length of mustard cord for the right-hand working cord. Aligning the cords at one end, tie them together with an overhand knot.

2. Take the right-hand working (mustard) cord and tie a right facing vertical lark's head knot over the static (white) cord, referring to Vertical Lark's Head Knot (Right Facing). Take the left-hand working (grey) cord and tie a left facing vertical lark's head knot over the static (white) cord, referring to Vertical Lark's Head Knot (Left Facing), ensuring it is secured directly beneath the knot above (A).

3. Continuing to alternate the vertical lark's head knots, make the next right facing knot approx. 4cm (1½in) from the previously tied knots. Once the knot has been tightened to the static (white) cord, slide the knot up to sit directly beneath the previously tied knots; this will create a loop from the right-hand working cord (B, C).

4. This time working with the left-hand working (grey) cord, repeat step 3 to make a left facing knot and loop (D).

5. Repeat steps 3 and 4 until you reach the end of the cord (E, F, G), then finish the sinnet by tying the ends with an overhand knot to secure.

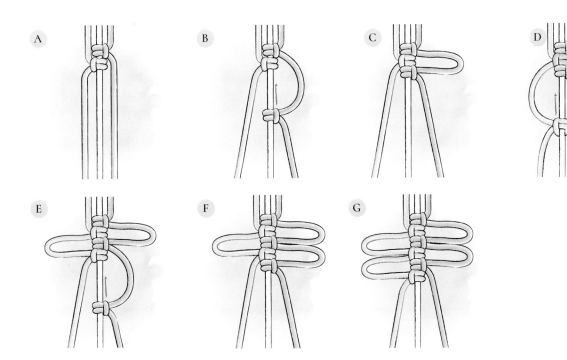

WRAP KNOT

The wrap knot, sometimes referred to as a constrictor knot, is a secure fastening used to bind multiple cords together, for keyring ends for example, or at the top of plant hangers. It can be decorative as well as functional. Tied from one long length of cord, you can create varying widths, and your cord choice can add a colour accent.

1. Take a long length of cord and lay it on the foundation cords to be wrapped, forming a long 'U' shape at one end of the cord, short end facing upwards. Bring the long tail behind the foundation cords and wrap it around the U-shaped loop (A).

2. Continue to wrap the working end of the cord around the U-shaped loop for at least four wraps (you can create many more depending on the length of your cord), but do not cover the bottom of the loop.

3. Once you have finished wrapping, pass the working end through the bottom of the loop. Then gently and gradually pull up the short cord end at the start of your wraps. The loop at the base of the wraps now functions as a lasso, shortening to capture the working tail end within the wraps (B).

4. Continue until the loop is hidden in the centre of the wrapped knot, then trim the cord ends (C).

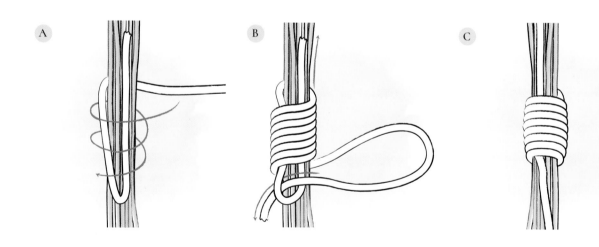

WRAP KNOT HANGING LOOP

The plant hanger is one of the most popular of macramé designs, and if you want to know my recommendation for how to start a plant hanger, it would be the wrap knot hanging loop. While they can be started with a metal hoop (see Getting Started), the wrap knot hanging loop is a much stronger option.

1. Fold your cord lengths in half and mark the halfway point with some clear sellotape, and lay them out horizontally across your lap or worktop. Take an additional long length of cord and tie a wrap knot across the sellotape with at least 10–20 wraps. For the example shown, I have used a 230cm (7½ft) length of cord to make a wrap knot with 36 wraps (A, B).

2. Fold the wrap knot in half to form a loop and use a shorter length of cord to tie a second wrap knot beneath the first, to join the ends of the first wrap knot together (C, D, E). For the example shown, I have used a 100cm (3¼ft) length of cord to make a wrap knot with nine wraps.

3. Once the wrap knot hanging loop is complete, cut the excess lengths of working cord (F).

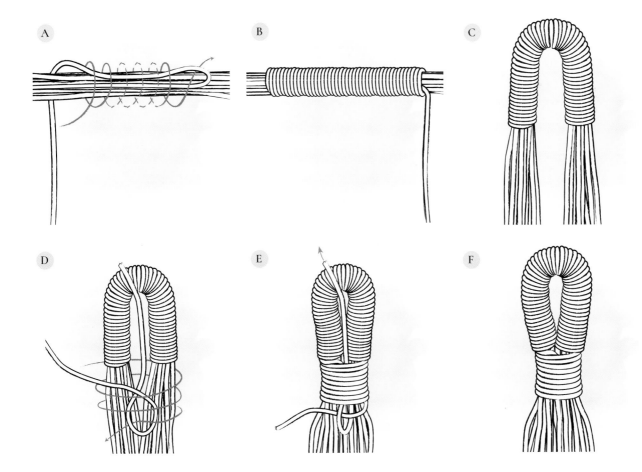

BRAIDS

Most people recognize a three-strand braid (or plait) and are familiar with the technique of passing cords over and under each other in order to create a pattern, but things get even more interesting when more strands are introduced. In this chapter, first we'll look at the specific weaving patterns required to create flat woven braids using three, four, five or six strands, before moving on to explore the three-dimensional rope effect that can be achieved when making crown box braids. Use coloured cords to practise these techniques to make it easier to understand the weaves.

THREE-STRAND BRAID

These simple plaits are a good place to start before moving on to the more complex weaving methods required for four-strand and five-strand braids. Start by gathering the three cords together and use an overhand knot to join them at one end.

1. Take the outside left cord and cross it over the middle cord (A).

2. Take the outside right cord and cross it over the middle cord (B).

3. Continue along the length of the cords repeating steps 1 and 2, alternating outside left into the middle with outside right into the middle. Continue until the braid is the length you desire (C).

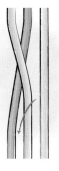

FOUR-STRAND BRAID

This braid is easier to practise and understand when using coloured cords in pairs. Begin by tying four different coloured cords onto a wooden ring or small dowel using a forward facing lark's head knot (see Single-Strand Knots) to give you four pairs of cords, and work each pair as it if was a single cord.

1. Take the first and third pair of cords (cords 1 and 3) and move each over the pairs of cords to their right (cords 2 and 4) (A).

2. Take the first pair of cords that was moved (cord 1, now in the second position) and weave it under the cord to its right (cord 4) (B). This completes the two-step weaving movement.

3. Continue tying the braid by repeating steps 1 and 2 on the cords now in the first and third positions (cords 2 and 4 move over cords 1 and 3, then cord 2 weaves under cord 3) (C, D).

4. Continue in this way until the braid is the desired length, remembering the two-step weaving movement, which can be summarized as

follows: move first and third cords over one cord to the right, then continue to move first cord only under the cord to its right.

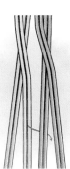

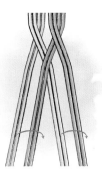

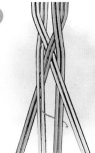

FIVE-STRAND BRAID

Five-strand braids might appear complex but all that is required is a two-step weave. Begin by tying five different coloured cords onto a wooden ring or small dowel using a forward facing lark's head knot (see Single-Strand Knots) to give you five pairs of cords, and work each pair as it if was a single cord.

1. Take the outside pairs of cords (cords 1 and 5) and move them over their neighbouring pairs of cords (cords 2 and 4) to be either side of the middle pair of cords (cord 3) (A).

2. Take the first cord that was moved (cord 1, now in the second position) and weave it under the middle cord (cord 3) and over the next cord, to take up its new position, second from last to the right (B). This completes the two-step weaving movement.

3. Continue tying the braid by repeating steps 1 and 2, remembering the two-step weaving movement, which can be summarized as follows: bring the outside cords in to be either side of the middle cord, then weave the left-hand cord under the middle cord and over the next cord to the right (C, D).

4. Continue until the braid is the length you desire (E).

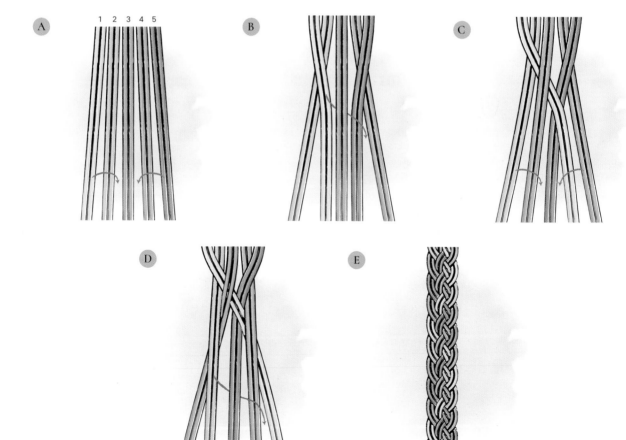

SIX-STRAND BRAID

Although you have more cords to work with when making a six-strand braid, the weaving pattern is very easy to remember. Starting with the left-hand cord, you simply weave it over and under the other cords in turn. Begin by tying six different coloured cords onto a wooden ring or small dowel using a forward facing lark's head knot (see Single-Strand Knots) to give you six pairs of cords, and work each pair as it if was a single cord.

1. Take the first pair of cords (cord 1) and weave it diagonally across each of the other pair of cords (cords 2 to 6) in an over, under, over, under, over pattern (A). Once the weave is complete cord 1 will be the last cord.

2. Take the new first cord (cord 2) and repeat the weaving pattern in step 1, to finish on the right-hand side as the last cord (B).

3. Repeat the weaving pattern as described in step 1 for the remaining four cords, and continue until the braid is the length you desire (C, D).

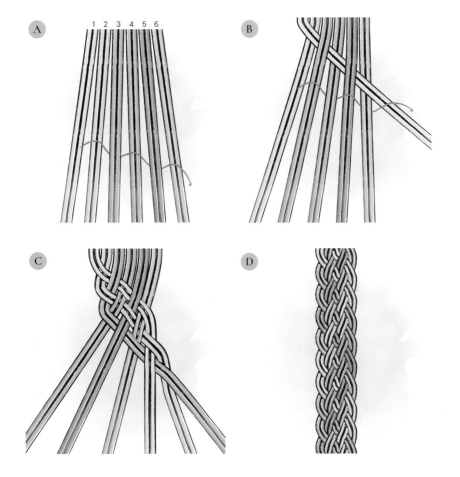

THREE-STRAND CROWN BOX BRAID

Crown box braids are a way to weave cords together to make a three-dimensional structure, a technique commonly seen when making macramé jewellery, particularly bracelets. Once joined, the cords are reorientated so you are working 'above' them, creating each round in a clockwise direction. The three-strand crown box braid has a slightly rounded profile. For demonstration purposes three different colours of cord are used; these are folded to give you three coloured cord pairs and each pair is worked as if it is a single cord.

1. Take three cords of equal length in different colours, fold in half and join together close to the fold point using an overhand knot (see Single-Strand Knots) to give you three pairs of cords.

2. Flatten out the top of the overhand knot as much as possible onto a work surface separating out the cords beneath so that cord 1 is placed vertically upwards, cord 2 horizontally to the right and cord 3 vertically downwards.

3. Fold cord 1 over cord 2 to create an open loop shape (A).

4. Fold cord 2 over cord 1, again making an open loop shape, with the tail resting over cord 3. Fold cord 3 over cord 2, and over and under cord 1, through the first loop made, to complete a round (B, C).

5. To fasten the round, pull all cords evenly (D, E). Continue to work rounds in a clockwise direction to the end of the cord lengths (F).

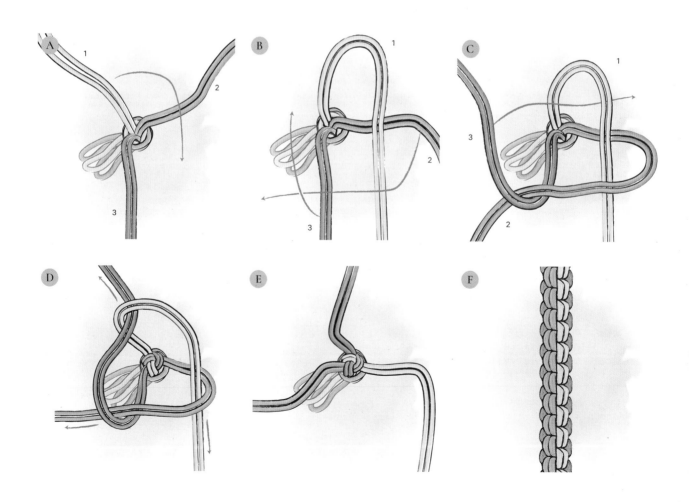

FOUR-STRAND CROWN BOX BRAID

The four-strand crown box braid has a squarer profile than the three-strand version, making it ideal for items such as pull cords. It is worked in a similar way, too, where the cords are rested over each other in a clockwise direction before weaving the last cord over and under the first cord to secure the round, so be sure to take note of the beginning cord of each round.

1. Take four cords of equal length and join together using an overhand knot. Flatten out the top of the overhand knot as much as possible onto a work surface separating out the cords beneath in an 'X' shape.

2. Fold cord 1 over cord 2 to create an open loop shape (A), and continue to work around clockwise creating an open curved loop with each cord, with the tail resting over the next cord, until you reach cord 4.

3. Fold cord 4 over cord 3 making an open loop shape, and over and under cord 1, through the first loop made, to complete the round (B). To fasten the round, pull all cords evenly (C).

4. Continue to work rounds in a clockwise direction until you reach the end of the cord lengths (D). Fasten with an overhand knot if desired.

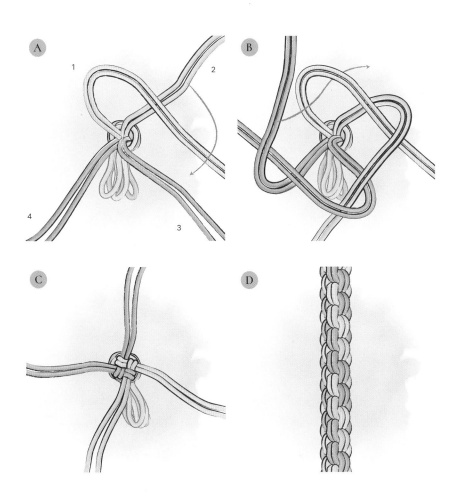

SQUARE KNOTS

Square knots are a staple for any macramé artist. Two half knots, when tied using mirroring actions in opposite directions, form a secure square knot, so it is a good idea to practise and learn the half knot and its variations first! Square knots are versatile for pattern designing: they can be tied above or below each other and also between knots on the row above. The key to understanding the square knot and its variations comes from understanding the relationship between the first and second step of tying the knot. This chapter explains how to tie the family of knots related to the square knot.

HALF KNOT

The half knot forms the first step in making a square knot, where it is tied around a pair of static cords as shown. However, it is also used to join cords, when tying diagonal half hitch diamonds for example, and in these instances it is not worked around static cords, but the tying process is just the same.

1. Working with four hanging cords, take the left-hand cord, cord 1, and place it across the other hanging cords, cords 2 to 4, then take the right-hand cord, cord 4, and lift it over the tail of cord 1 (A).

2. Take cord 4 and weave it under cords 2 and 3, pulling the tail out and through the space between cords 1 and 2 (B).

3. Pull the ends of cords 1 and 4 until the knot is in the desired place.

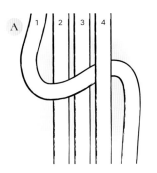
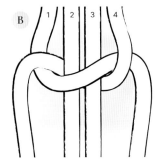

HALF KNOT SPIRAL

Half knot spirals are very easy to tie and create a lovely helix style pattern, great for making macramé key chains, plant hangers and, as details, in wall hangings.

1. Working with four hanging cords and starting with the cord on the left-hand side, cord 1, tie a half knot (A).

2. Repeat step 1 to tie another half knot, again starting with the left-hand cord, which is now cord 4, and pull the two working cords so the knot sits directly beneath the one above (B).

3. Repeat steps 1 and 2 to continue tying half knots, always remembering to start with the left-hand cord first (C).

4. If all your knots are tied the same, they will naturally start to spiral, and the more knots you tie the more you will be able to twist them after tying to create a tighter or looser spiral (D).

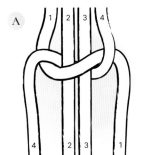
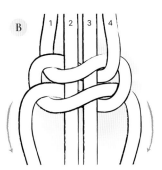
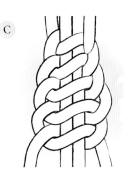
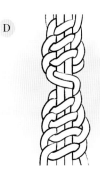

TWO-COLOUR HALF KNOT SPIRAL

A two-colour half knot spiral is made by tying a half knot spiral using two different colour cords for the working cords, switching between colours as the spiral is tied. Be sure to pay careful attention to the position of the colour cords before tying the half knots.

1. Working with four hanging cords in colour 1, tie a half knot.

2. Next take a length of your colour 2 cord, fold it in half and place the midway point directly beneath the first half knot, making sure that the working cords of colour 1 are lying on top of colour 2 (A).

3. Tie a half knot using colour 1 working cords; this secures the new colour cord in place (B, C).

4. Now tie a half knot with colour 2 working cords, but first make sure the left-hand cord is **under** the colour 1 working cord and that the right-hand cord is **over** the colour 1 working cord (D). Then use the colour 1 working cords to tie a half knot, making sure that the cords are placed as before, i.e. that the left-hand cord is **under** the colour 2 working cord and that the right-hand cord is **over** the colour 2 working cord.

5. Repeat step 4 to continue to tie half knots, alternating the working cord colours and paying particular attention to the position of the working cords (E, F, G).

6. The spiral will begin to naturally occur as you tie the knots, but to avoid confusion try to keep it as flat as possible as you work, then twist it at the end to see the final result (H, I).

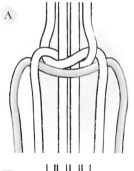

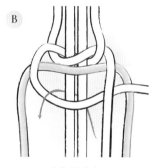

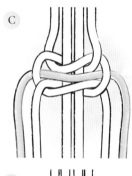

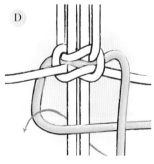

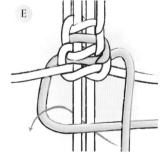

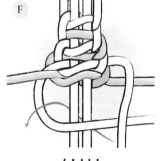

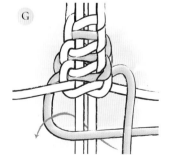

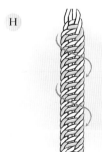

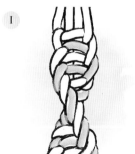

SQUARE KNOT (LEFT FACING)

The basic square knot is worked over four hanging cords with the working cords on the outside. It's a two-step tying process and the second step mirrors the first. For a square knot with a loop on the left-hand side, start with the left-hand cord.

1. Take the left-hand cord, cord 1, and place across cords 2, 3 and 4 at a right angle, then take cord 4 and place it over cord 1 (A). Leaving cord 1 in place, move cord 4 behind cords 2 and 3, pulling its tail through the space between cords 1 and 2. Pull on cords 1 and 4 to complete a half knot (B).

2. Mirroring step 1, take the right-hand cord, cord 1, across the other cords. Take the left-hand cord, cord 4, and place it over cord 1 (C). Leaving cord 1 in place, move cord 4 behind cords 2 and 3, pulling it through the space at the bottom of the loop to create a half knot facing in the opposite direction.

3. Pull on the working cords, cords 1 and 4, and the bottom half knot will secure below the first to complete the square knot (D).

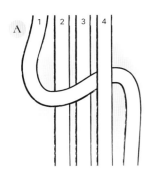
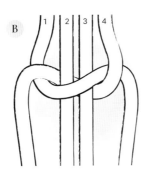
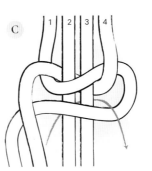
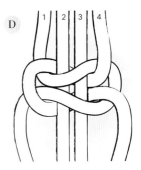

SQUARE KNOT (RIGHT FACING)

Right facing square knots have a loop on the right-hand side, and you will start the two-step mirrored tying action with the cord on the right-hand side. If left-hand dominant you may find this version of the square knot a more natural fit.

1. Take the right-hand cord, cord 4, and place across cords 3, 2 and 1 at a right angle, then take cord 1 and place it over cord 4 (A). Leaving cord 4 in place, move cord 1 behind cords 2 and 3, pulling its tail through the space between cords 3 and 4. Pull on cords 1 and 4 to complete a half knot (B).

2. Mirroring step 1, take the left-hand cord, cord 4, across the other cords. Take the right-hand cord, cord 1, and place it over cord 4 (C). Leaving cord 4 in place, move cord 1 behind cords 3 and 2, pulling it through the space at the bottom of the loop to create a half knot facing in the opposite direction.

3. Pull on the working cords, cords 1 and 4, and the bottom half knot will secure below the first to complete the square knot (D).

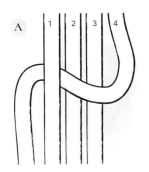
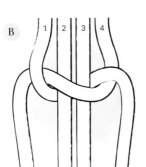
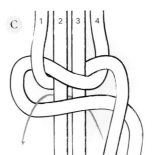
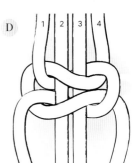

ALTERNATING SQUARE KNOTS

By alternating cords when tying square knots, you can start to build up interesting patterns including geometric shapes such as triangles and diamonds. It is important to ensure that each square knot is tied facing the same way (either all left facing, as shown, or all right facing) to avoid spiralling.

1. Starting with eight cords, tie two square knots, the first using cords 1 to 4 and the second using cords 5 to 8 (A).

2. Now working with two cords from each of the square knots tied in the first row, cords 3 and 4 and cords 5 and 6, tie a square knot on a new row, noting that cords 3 and 6 will be your working cords (B).

3. On the next row, tie two square knots as in step 1, the first using cords 1 to 4 and the second using cords 5 to 8 (C).

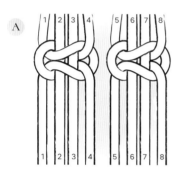
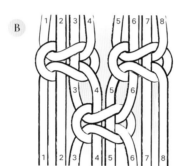
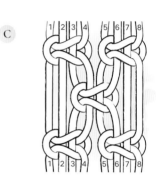

SQUARE KNOT PICOT SINNET

Looping square knots can be used to make fun ornaments, or to create a textured wall hanging when displayed together in multiples. With this technique, loops of cord, or 'picots', are created between the square knots.

1. Starting with four cords, tie a square knot, then allowing for a space in between, tie a second square knot (A). Continue to tie square knots one beneath the other, leaving spaces in between. In the example shown, I have chosen to increase the spaces between my knots so that the loops get progressively larger.

2. Once all knots are tied, close up in between spaces, as indicated in (A), to create the loops. Starting from the top, slide each knot up to sit beneath the one above it to create a loop at either side: hold onto cords 2 and 3 in your non-dominant hand as you pinch the square knot with the index finger and thumb of your dominant hand, sliding it upwards (B, C).

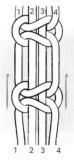

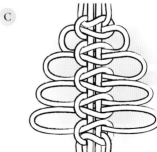

BERRY KNOT

Berry knots are three-dimensional knots that create a raised round bobble effect when included in projects. They are created from a square knot sinnet.

1. Tie four square knots one beneath the other to form a sinnet. Take the outside working cords, cords 1 and 4, and lift them up and through the corresponding spaces at the top of the sinnet (A).

2. Now take the inner cords, cords 2 and 3, and lift them up and through the space between cords 2 and 3 at the top of the sinnet, pulling cord 2 through to the left and cord 3 through to the right (B).

3. Pull down the cords at either side to lift the sinnet up to form the rounded berry shape (C, D).

4. Secure the berry knot by tying one more square knot at its base (E).

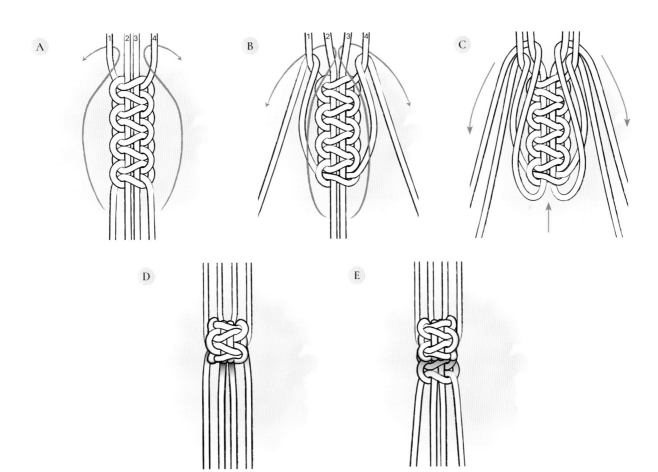

HALF HITCH KNOTS

Half hitches (or clove hitches) are tied in two distinct ways, either as single half hitches or as double half hitches. Single half hitches, often referred to by the way in which the cords are facing (i.e. left or right) make decorative but unsecured loops. More often seen are double half hitches, where two half hitches are tied alongside each other, and mastering tying them in all directions – vertically, horizontally and diagonally – is essential. The lines of loops they create are used to describe geometric shapes in patterns.

HALF HITCH (LEFT FACING)

A single half hitch is rarely seen alone, but examining the simple tying movement it requires in isolation is essential for success in tying the knots in combination. Let's start with a left facing half hitch.

1. Working with two cords, loop the right-hand working cord around the left-hand static cord, bringing the working cord back over itself (A, B).

2. Pull the working cord down to finish the knot (C). (Note: a single half hitch is not secure.)

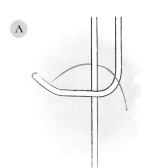 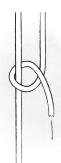 

HALF HITCH (RIGHT FACING)

Now let's look at mirroring the tying movement required to produce the right facing half hitch.

1. Working with two cords, loop the left-hand working cord around the right-hand static cord, bringing the working cord back over itself (A, B).

2. Pull the working cord down to finish the knot (C). (Note: a single half hitch is not secure.)

 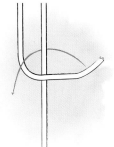  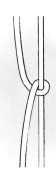

ALTERNATING HALF HITCHES

This sinnet is created by alternating left facing half hitch knots with right facing half hitch knots, as the cords take it in turn to be the working cord. It's a useful technique to practise tying the half hitch knots in different directions to reinforce muscle memory.

1. First tie a left facing half hitch knot, then mirror your actions to tie a right facing half hitch knot (A, B).

2. Repeat step 1, tying a left facing half hitch knot followed by a right facing half hitch knot, to create an alternating pattern, and continue until the sinnet is the length you desire (C, D).

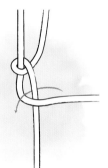
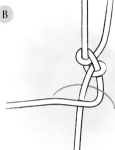
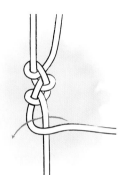

HALF HITCH SPIRAL

Half hitch knots all tied to face the same way, either all to the left as seen here, or all to the right, can be repeated one after the other to create a sinnet with a wrapped effect that spirals around one or more bound cords. The half hitch spiral is often seen on plant hangers.

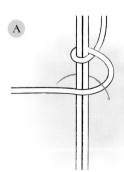

1. Measure and cut a static cord or cords a little longer than you want the finished spiral to be. Cut a long working cord with which to bind the static cords – spiral knots use a lot of working cord so six times the length of the spiral is a good starting point. Tie the working cord around the static cords using a left facing half hitch (A).

2. Make another left facing half hitch with the working cord, securing it directly below the one above (B).

3. Repeat step 2 to continue to tie left facing half hitch knots around your static cords. The spiral will begin to naturally occur as you tie the knots, but to avoid confusion try to keep it as flat as possible when tying the knots, then twist it at the end (C, D). Fasten with an overhand knot if desired.

VERTICAL DOUBLE HALF HITCHES

Vertical double half hitches are a way of adding a length of cord onto a hanging static cord or cords. They are tied in rows. In the example shown, I have used grey for the hanging cords and white for the working cord, for the sake of clarity.

1. Working from left to right, the first double half hitch tied will fasten the working cord to the first pair of hanging cords. Making sure the working cord is horizontal to the vertical hanging cords, wrap it behind and around the hanging cords and bring it down behind itself to create the first loop (A).

2. Create a second loop in the same way, again wrapping the working cord behind and around the hanging cords and bringing it down behind itself. Pull on the working cord to bring the loops together, securing the double half hitch knot around the hanging cords (B, C).

3. Repeat steps 1 and 2 to tie a double half hitch knot on the next pair of hanging cords (D, E), and continue in this way to complete a row of vertical double half hitch knots (F).

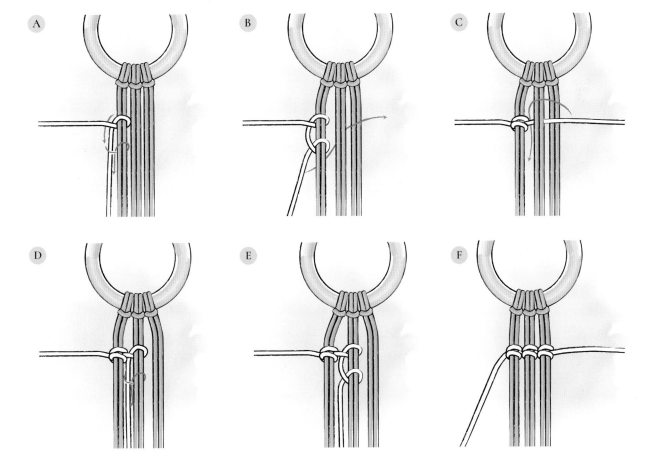

COLOUR CHANGES USING VERTICAL DOUBLE HALF HITCHES

Many projects rely on the secure nature of the vertical double half hitch knot to allow different cord colours to be added when creating pixel-style patterns. This example shows how to introduce a new cord colour in the middle of a row of vertical double half hitches.

1. When you reach the point where the new colour is to be added, cut a long length of cord and temporarily fasten one end of it alongside your cast on cords. Bring the new colour cord down to the relevant hanging cords and tie a vertical double half hitch knot (A, B).

2. Once the first knot is secured, you can untie the cast on cord. Continue to tie as many vertical double half hitch knots using the new colour as the pattern requires, in this case a total of two, then bring the original working cord behind the new colour knots and use it to continue to tie vertical double half hitch knots to the end of the row (C).

3. Leave the new colour working cords in place and, if the colour pattern continues on subsequent rows, carry the cords behind the project as they are needed.

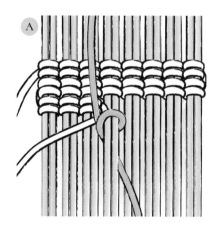

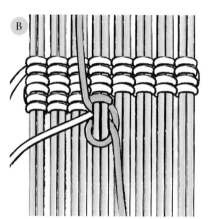

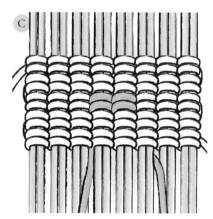

HORIZONTAL DOUBLE HALF HITCHES

Horizontal double half hitches are created in a similar way to diagonal double half hitches, usually from existing hanging cords, as shown here, although they can be used to add a new length of cord. First identify the cord or cords the knots will be tied onto, shown as grey in this example. These will become static cords and need to be held under tension horizontally as horizontal double half hitches are tied around them using the remaining hanging cords.

1. On this example, cords 1 and 2 are going to become static cords with a horizontal orientation to the right; working from left to right, hold cords 1 and 2 horizontally across the other hanging cords.

2. Take cord 3 and tie a double half hitch knot onto the horizontally held static cords (A).

3. Repeat step 2 with each of the hanging cords in turn until you reach the end of the row (B, C).

 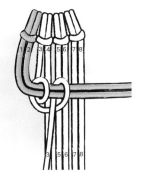 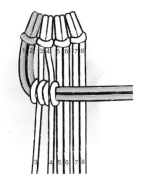 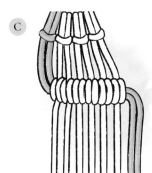

DIAGONAL DOUBLE HALF HITCHES

Diagonal double half hitches are tied using existing hanging cords. First identify the cord or pair of cords that the knots are to be tied onto, shown as grey in this example. These will become static cords. Tension is important here and, by holding the static cords diagonally, it helps ensure that the tied knots are placed correctly.

1. On this example, cords 1 and 2 are going to become static cords with a diagonal orientation down to the right; working from left to right, hold cords 1 and 2 diagonally to the right.

2. Take cord 3 and tie a double half hitch knot onto the diagonally held static cords (A).

3. Repeat step 2 with each of the hanging cords in turn (B, which shows a double half hitch being tied with cord 5).

4. When all the hanging cords have been tied onto the static cords, you will have created a diagonal line of loops (C).

 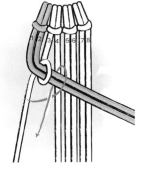  

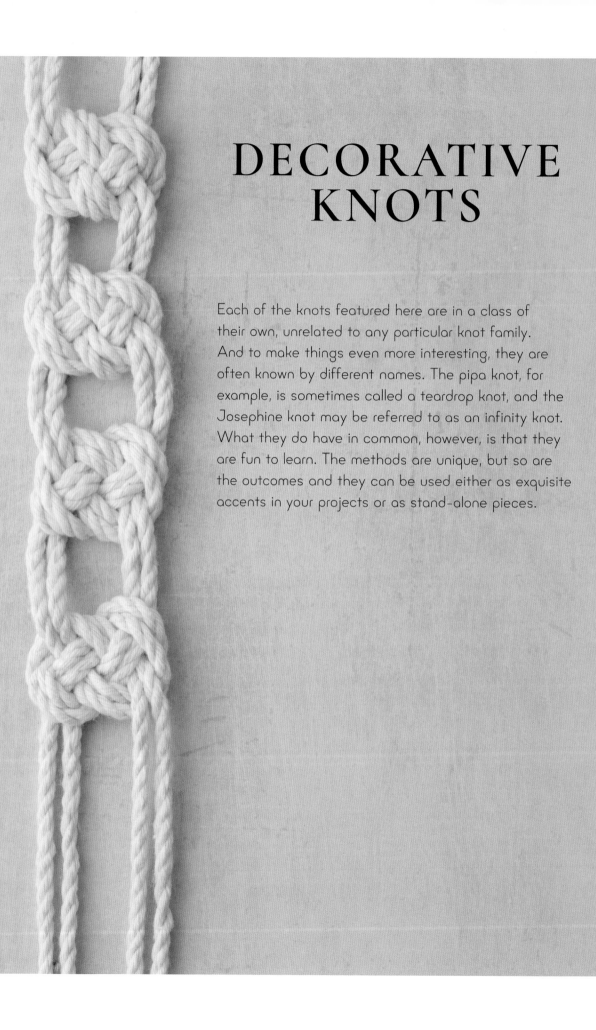

DECORATIVE KNOTS

Each of the knots featured here are in a class of their own, unrelated to any particular knot family. And to make things even more interesting, they are often known by different names. The pipa knot, for example, is sometimes called a teardrop knot, and the Josephine knot may be referred to as an infinity knot. What they do have in common, however, is that they are fun to learn. The methods are unique, but so are the outcomes and they can be used either as exquisite accents in your projects or as stand-alone pieces.

JOSEPHINE KNOT

The Josephine knot loops and weaves hanging cords together to create an elegant infinity-style knot, for a decorative focal point that can be used to great effect in wall hangings and plant hangers. This example shows the tying of the knot using two pairs of cords in grey and white, for maximum clarity.

1. Take the right-hand (white) pair of hanging cords and create a 'd' shape loop with the tail lengths facing horizontally across to the right (A).

2. Take the left-hand (grey) pair of hanging cords and create a 'b' shape loop with the tail lengths facing horizontally across to the left. The b-shape loop should be resting on top of and just below the d-shape loop (B).

3. Take the tails of the right-hand (white) cords and weave them in a diagonal direction over the grey cords, under the white cords, then back over the grey cords (C).

4. Then take the tail of the grey cords and pass them under the white loop (D).

5. Pull the cords gently and evenly to form the knot (E, F).

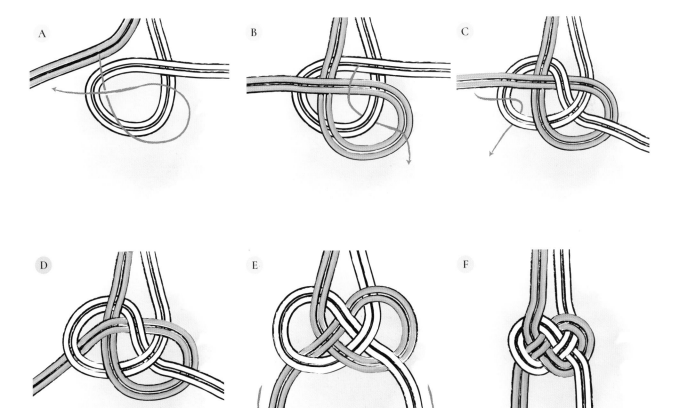

PIPA KNOT

Often seen on key chains or as the focal point of a necklace, a pipa knot is made by manipulating a single length of cord around a loop established at the top of the knot. It's simple to make and looks simply great! It can help to fasten the non-working end of the cord to your table with masking tape.

1. Fasten one end of the cord to your work top with masking tape. Create a small loop with the working end of the cord, resting the long tail to the bottom right (A).

2. Continue to move the long tail around to the left to create a bottom-heavy figure of eight shape, resting the tail to the top right. Note: the size of the bottom loop will dictate the maximum size of the finished knot; I recommend making it approx. twice the size of the top loop (B).

3. Now continue to wrap the tail length tightly behind the back of the top loop and bring it back down to form another loop within the bottom loop, making it slightly smaller so that it fits within it comfortably (C).

4. Bring the tail length around behind the top loop, pulling it tight to the loop, and back down once more to repeat step 3, making one final loop within the bottom loops (D, E).

5. Take the tail length around behind the top loop once again, pulling it tight to the loop, then bring it down through the gap in the smallest of the bottom loops and out at the base of the formed knot. Trim the ends to finish (F, G).

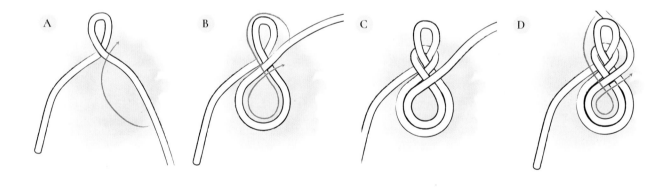

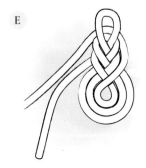

DAISY CHAIN SINNET

A daisy chain sinnet, sometimes known as just a chain sinnet, allows you to make a decorative braid out of a single cord, where loops are joined across its length to create a chain effect. It's particularly fast to work, which makes it very satisfying.

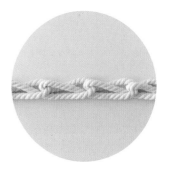

1. Place your cord horizontally making a loop at one end (A).

2. Create a 'U' shape bend in the working length and pinch it between your index finger and thumb to pass it down through the loop, pulling it out horizontally to the right-hand side to complete the formation of the foundation loop (B, C).

3. Again, make a U-shape with the working length, and pinch it to push it through the previous loop, pulling it out to the right-hand side to make the next horizontally orientated loop (D, E).

4. Repeat step 3 to create a chain of your desired length (F) (you are aiming for evenly spaced loops), then take the working cord through the final loop to secure this end of the chain (G). Return to the starting end of the chain and pull the tail of the first loop tight to secure it at the other end.

A   B   C   D

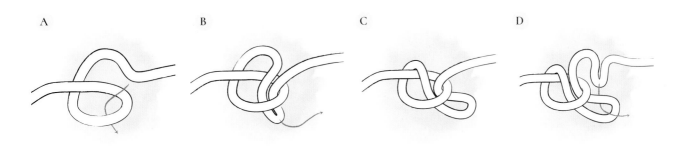

E   F   G

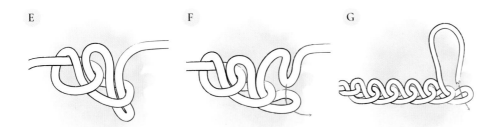

LEAF KNOT

A leaf knot is often seen in macramé jewellery projects, particularly necklaces made from extra-chunky cord, although it could also be used as a feature on single hanging cords in a wall hanging. It has the appearance of a three-strand braid but is worked from just one length of cord.

1. Place the cord length horizontally and create a small loop at one end by bringing the tail under the cord, then take the tail end down and back up to make a large loop hanging down, passing the tail through the small loop (A).

2. Take the working (horizontally orientated) end of the cord and weave it through the large loop, passing it under then over from left to right, and under then over from right to left (B, C).

3. Continue to weave the working end around the vertical cords as described in step 2, creating a herringbone effect (D, E).

4. Continue until most of the working cord is used up, then take the tail ends and gently pull in opposite directions to tighten the loops and form the knot's shape (F).

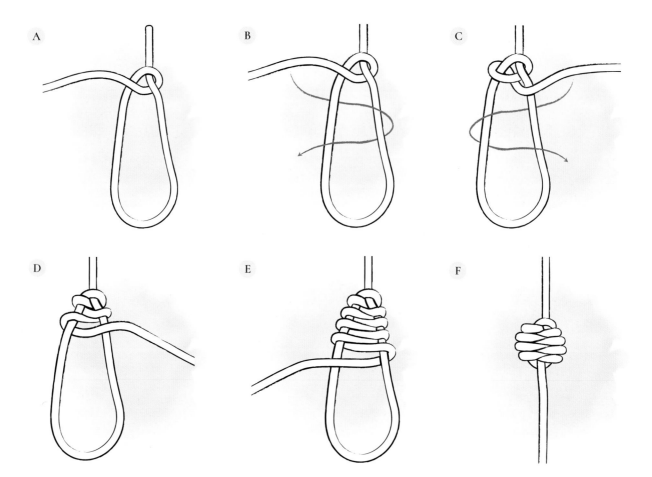

RAIN KNOT SINNET

A rain knot joins two cords together with an interlocked appearance and is particularly effective when tied with two different colours. Rain knot sinnets are often encountered in macramé jewellery designs, for making bracelets and necklaces.

1. Working with two hanging cords, take the right-hand cord around the left-hand cord, bringing the right-hand cord back over itself to form a loop (A).

2. Making sure that the tail of the right-hand cord is resting over the left-hand cord, bring the tail of the left-hand cord up to pass it through the loop in the right-hand cord (B).

3. Pull down on the ends of both cords to produce the interlocking pair of loops that forms the finished knot (C).

4. Repeat steps 1 to 3 to continue to tie rain knots, each as close to the one before as possible, to create a sinnet (D).

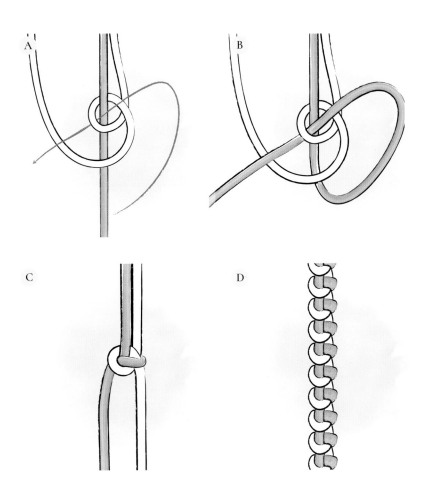

NET
PATTERNS

Each of the samples in this section gives you an opportunity to practise square knots and to discover how by varying their placement, or the placement of the cords within them, you can create net patterns that have various woven effects. We'll start with a simple alternating square knot and finish with a fishtail weave that looks more complex than it actually is! Each net pattern begins in the same way, by creating a loop of foundation cord to work onto, which is then secured to a macramé board (see Essential Skills: Project Set-Up) or to a cork board with pins. Once the macramé is complete, simply use the foundation cord loop to hang the project up.

ALTERNATING DOUBLE SQUARE KNOTS

This simple pattern utilizes the alternating square knot technique seen in Square Knots but with the added twist of doubling up square knots before switching the knot placement on each row to alternate them.

MATERIALS

- One 60cm (24in) length of 3mm (⅛in) macramé cord
- Eight 120cm (47in) lengths of 3mm (⅛in) macramé cord
- Mini macramé board or cork board and pins

FINISHED SIZE

Width: 15cm (6in)
Length: 18cm (7in) for knotted section

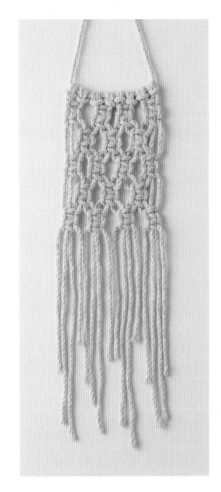

1. Take the 60cm (24in) cord length, and join the ends together with a securely tied overhand knot (see Single-Strand Knots) to form a loop. This is your foundation cord. With the knot centred above the board, secure it to the board to give you a length of cord to work onto measuring approx. 15cm (6in).

2. Take the eight 120cm (47in) cord lengths, fold each in half and attach them to the foundation cord using forward lark's head knots (see Single-Strand Knots), to give you sixteen working cords (A). Working in rows, continue as follows.

3. **Row 1:** Take the first four hanging cords and tie a square knot. Continue to tie square knots across all working cords to complete the row (four square knots in total).

4. **Row 2:** Tie four more square knots directly beneath the knots created in the row above (B).

5. **Row 3 and 4:** Pushing aside two working cords to either side, work only on the twelve central cords. Take the first four cords and tie an alternating square knot, joining two cords from each of the knots in the row above. Continue to tie square knots across the remaining cords to complete the row (three square knots in total). Tie three more square knots directly below the knots created in row 3 (C).

6. **Rows 5-10:** Repeat rows 1 to 4, then finish by repeating rows 1 and 2 once more.

7. Once the pattern is complete, remove from the board and trim fringe lengths as preferred.

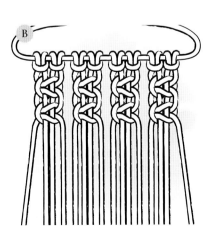

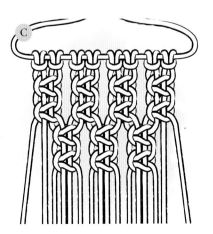

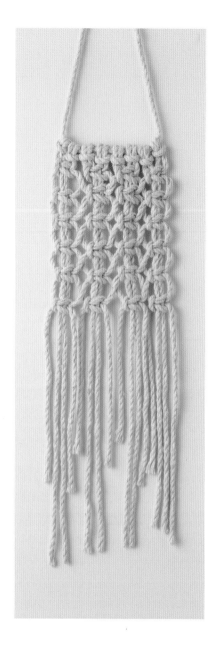

CROSSOVER CORDS SQUARE KNOTS

This pattern has rows of square knots all placed on the same static cords but the working cords from neighbouring square knots on the row above are continuously switching to give the crossover effect between the rows.

MATERIALS

- One 60cm (24in) length of 3mm (⅛in) macramé cord
- Eight 120cm (47in) lengths of 3mm (⅛in) macramé cord
- Mini macramé board or cork board and pins

FINISHED SIZE

Width: 15cm (6in)
Length: 16cm (6¼in) for knotted section

1. Take the 60cm (24in) cord length, and join the ends together with a securely tied overhand knot (see Single-Strand Knots) to form a loop. This is your foundation cord. With the knot centred above the board, secure it to the board to give you a length of cord to work onto measuring approx. 15cm (6in).

2. Take the eight 120cm (47in) cord lengths, fold each in half and attach them to the foundation cord using forward lark's head knots (see Single-Strand Knots), to give you sixteen working cords (A). Working in rows, continue as follows.

3. **Row 1:** Take the first four hanging cords and tie a square knot. Continue to tie square knots across all working cords to complete the first row (four square knots in total) (B).

4. **Row 2:** For the next row (and all subsequent rows), you will be tying square knots underneath the square knots on the row above, but you will be switching the working cords for each knot as described in the following steps.

5. First knot: For your working cords, use cord 1 but leave cord 4 hanging and pick up cord 5 (the first working cord of the next knot on the row above) and tie the first square knot (C).

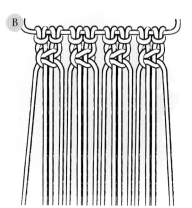

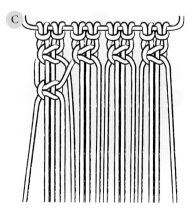

6. Middle of row knots: To tie these square knots, take as your working cords the last working cord from the previous knot on the row above and the first working cord from the next knot on the row above, so creating the crossover cord effect (D). Tie two square knots like this.

7. Final knot: To tie the last square knot of the row, take as your working cords the last working cord from the previous knot on the row above and the last working cord from the knot directly above (cord 16) (E).

8. Row 3: Repeat steps 4–7 to tie a row of four square knots beneath the row above (F). You will begin to see the crossover pattern of the working cords between knots.

9. Rows 4–6: Repeating steps 4 to 7, tie another three rows, each with four square knots, to continue the crossover cords square knot pattern (G, shows row 4 completed).

10. Once the pattern is complete, remove the sample from the board and trim the fringe lengths as preferred.

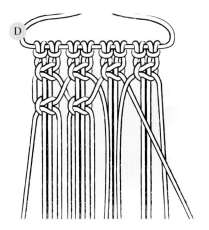

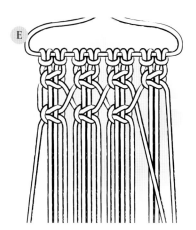

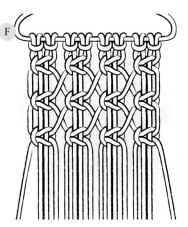

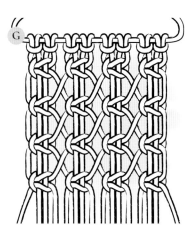

WOVEN FISHTAIL SQUARE KNOTS

This pattern has a complex appearance but the fishtail weave is easy to achieve with some careful counting. Columns of square knots are worked over the same static cords but the working cords are changed each time, working outwards from the centre, although the best way to understand the process is to give it a go!

MATERIALS

- One 60cm (24in) length of 3mm (⅛in) macramé cord
- Eight 120cm (47in) lengths of 3mm (⅛in) macramé cord
- Mini macramé board or cork board and pins

FINISHED SIZE

Width: 15cm (6in)

Length: 14cm (5½in) for knotted section

1. Take the 60cm (24in) cord length, and join the ends together with a securely tied overhand knot (see Single-Strand Knots) to form a loop. This is your foundation cord. With the knot centred above the board, secure it to the board to give you a length of cord to work onto measuring approx. 15cm (6in).

2. Take the eight 120cm (47in) cord lengths, fold each in half and attach them to the foundation cord using forward lark's head knots (see Single-Strand Knots), to give you sixteen working cords (A).

3. Divide the cords into two sets of eight and work on each set of cords in turn. Working on the left-hand set of eight cords, tie the first square knot with cords 3–6, using cords 4 and 5 as your static cords and cords 3 and 6 as your working cords (B).

4. Directly beneath, tie the second square knot over the same static cords (cords 4 and 5) but switching to cords 2 and 7 for the working cords (C).

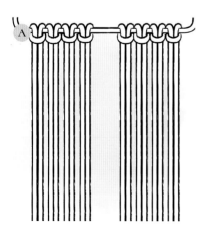

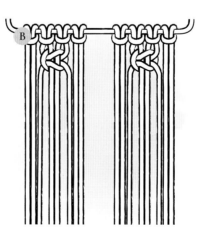

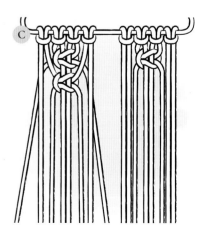

5. For the third and final square knot in the column, use cords 1 and 8 as your working cords to tie a square knot directly beneath, again around the same static cords (cords 4 and 5) (D).

6. Repeat steps 3 to 5 to tie a column of three square knots with the right-hand set of eight hanging cords, remembering to switch out your working cords each time to work your way outwards.

7. Once the first two columns of three square knots is complete, it's time to bring the two sets of cords together by working the next (central) column of three square knots using cords 5 to 8 from the left-hand set of cords and cords 1 to 4 from the right-hand set of cords as your new set of cords.

8. Selecting the middle four cords of your new set of eight cords, tie your first square knot (E).

9. Directly below, tie the second square knot around the same central two static cords, but this time selecting the next pair of cords outwards as your working cords (F).

10. For the third and final square knot in the central column, discard the working cords of the knot above and select the next two most outwardly cords as your working cords to tie around the central two static cords (G).

11. To complete the pattern, repeat steps 3 to 6 to tie the final two columns of three square knots. But here's a tip: it's easier to select the right cords for tying the first of the square knots if you count from the middle outwards. So, identify the middle four cords (these will not be tied), then tie a square knot with the next four cords to either side (H). Then work on the left-hand side to complete the left-hand column (I), before returning to complete the right-hand column

12. Once the pattern is complete, remove the sample from the board and trim the fringe lengths as preferred.

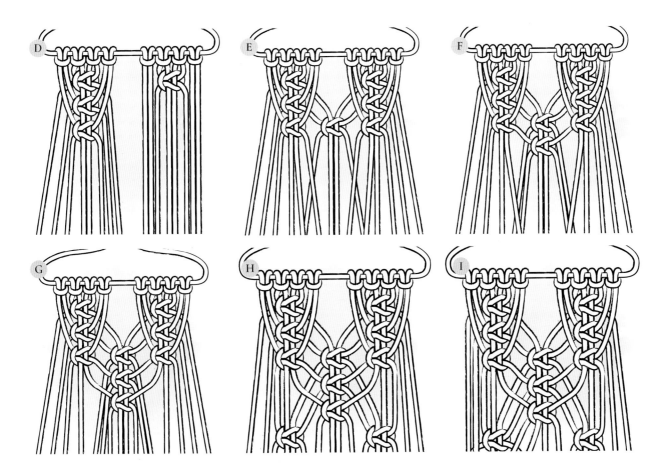

FOUR-CORD CHAINS

Each of the chains in this section are variations on a diagonal double half hitch (abbreviated to 'diagonal dhh') diamond pattern. We'll start first with the simple 'empty' diamond chain, then go on to explore how adding decorations such as rya tassels, or additional knots such as square knots, can develop a simple design, and we finish with the distinctively shaped fishtail chain. Each chain begins in the same way, by tying four lengths of cord onto a small wooden ring using forward lark's head knots to give you eight working cords. Once the macramé is complete, simply attach a loop of cord to the top of the ring to make a small hanging or door handle hanger.

DIAGONAL DHH DIAMOND CHAIN

Perfect the tying of diagonal double half hitch in both directions with this repeating diamond pattern chain.

MATERIALS

- Four 175cm (69in) lengths of 3mm (⅛in) macramé cord
- One 80cm (32in) length of 3mm (⅛in) macramé cord
- 5.5cm (2¼in) wooden ring

FINISHED SIZE

Width: 5cm (2in)
Length: 28cm (11in)

1. Take the four 175cm (69in) cord lengths, fold each in half and attach them onto the wooden ring using forward lark's head knots (see Single-Strand Knots), to give you eight working cords.

2. Take the middle two cords and join together with a half knot (see Square Knots) (A).

3. Working from the centre to the left, hold the left-hand cord diagonally to become a static cord. Tie diagonal double half hitch knots onto the static cord using the first three hanging cords (see Half Hitch Knots) (B).

4. Working from the centre to the right, mirror the actions of step 3, tying double half hitch knots onto the right-hand static cord using the last three hanging cords (C).

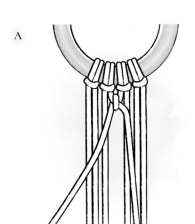

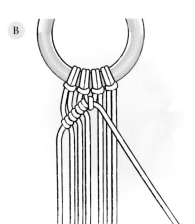

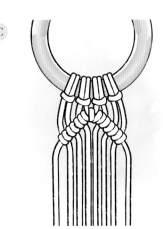

5. Return to the left-hand static cord and place it to the right to face diagonally towards the centre. Working from the left to the centre, tie diagonal double half hitch knots onto this cord using the first three hanging cords (D).

6. Now, returning to the right-hand static cord, place it to the left to face diagonally towards the centre. Working from the right to the centre, tie diagonal double half hitch knots onto this cord using the last three hanging cords, to complete the first diamond shape.

7. Where the static cords meet in the middle, join them together with a half knot to form the top knot of the next diamond (E).

8. Repeat steps 3 to 7 to create another diamond shape beneath the first (F). You have sufficient cord to make a chain of four repeating diamonds (G).

9. To finish, bundle the working cords together and fasten with a wrap knot made from the remaining 80cm (32in) length of cord (see Single-Strand Knots), trimming the ends to the same length (H).

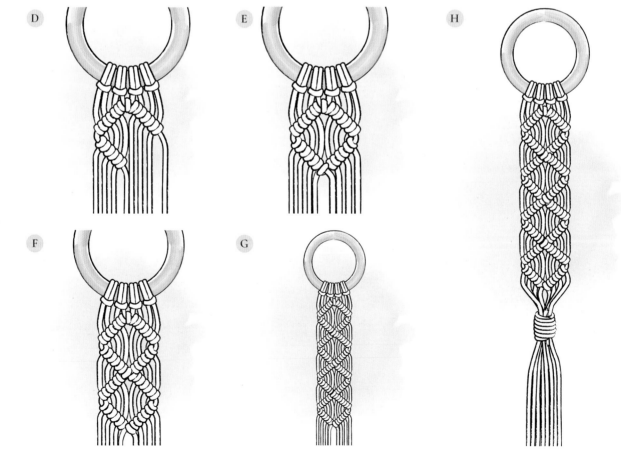

RYA TASSELS

Rya tassels are a great addition to fill the 'empty' space in the middle of the diamonds in a diagonal double half hitch diamond chain. They are created by weaving a bundle of cords through the vertical cords that run through the centre of the diamond shapes.

MATERIALS

- Six 18cm (7in) lengths of 3mm (⅛in) macramé cord for the rya tassels

FINISHED SIZE

Width: 5cm (2in)

Length: 28cm (11in)

1. First make a diagonal double half hitch diamond chain ready to add your rya tassel decorations to (see Diagonal DHH Diamond Chain). Working on the diamond shape at the top of the completed chain, notice that there are four vertical cords. The cord bundle that creates the rya tassel will be tied around the middle two cords, numbered cords 4 and 5.

2. Take a bundle of three 18cm (7in) cords, lie them diagonally across the bottom of the diamond, and tuck the ends under cord 4 (A).

3. Bring the ends back over cords 4 and 5 to the right, creating a loop, and now tuck the ends under cord 5 to come back up between cords 4 and 5 (B).

4. Pull down on the tails of the bundle to secure the rya tassel, then trim as desired (C).

5. Repeat steps 2 to 4 to tie a second rya tassel in the centre of the third diamond shape using the remaining three cord lengths.

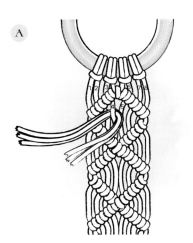

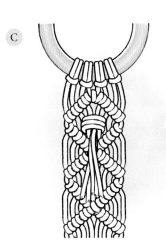

DIAGONAL DHH DIAMOND CHAIN WITH SQUARE KNOTS

In this variation of the diagonal double half hitch diamond chain, the diamond shapes are top-and-tailed with rows of square knots, with a single square knot featured in the middle of each diamond shape too.

MATERIALS

- Four 175cm (69in) lengths of 3mm (⅛in) macramé cord
- One 80cm (32in) length of 3mm (⅛in) macramé cord
- 5.5cm (2¼in) wooden ring

FINISHED SIZE

Width: 5cm (2in)

Length: 33cm (13in)

1. Take the four 175cm (69in) cord lengths, fold them in half and attach them onto the wooden ring using forward lark's head knots (see Single-Strand Knots), to give you eight working cords. Divide the cords into two sets of four and tie two square knots next to each other (see Square Knots) (A).

2. Below the square knots, identify the middle two cords and join them with a half knot (see Square Knots).

3. Now create the top half of the diamond shape, referring to Diagonal DHH Diamond Chain, steps 3 and 4 (B).

4. Identifying the middle four cords, tie a square knot below the top half of the diagonal double half hitch diamond (C).

5. Now create the bottom half of the diamond shape, referring to Diagonal DHH Diamond Chain, steps 5 and 6. Where the cords meet in the middle, join them together with a diagonal double half hitch knot to complete the diamond.

6. Divide the working cords into two sets of four and tie two square knots next to each other (D).

7. Repeat steps 2 to 6 twice more, to create a chain of three diamond shapes in total, ending with a row of two square knots.

8. To finish, bundle the working cords together and fasten with a wrap knot made from the remaining 80cm (32in) length of cord (see Single-Strand Knots), trimming the ends to be the same length (E).

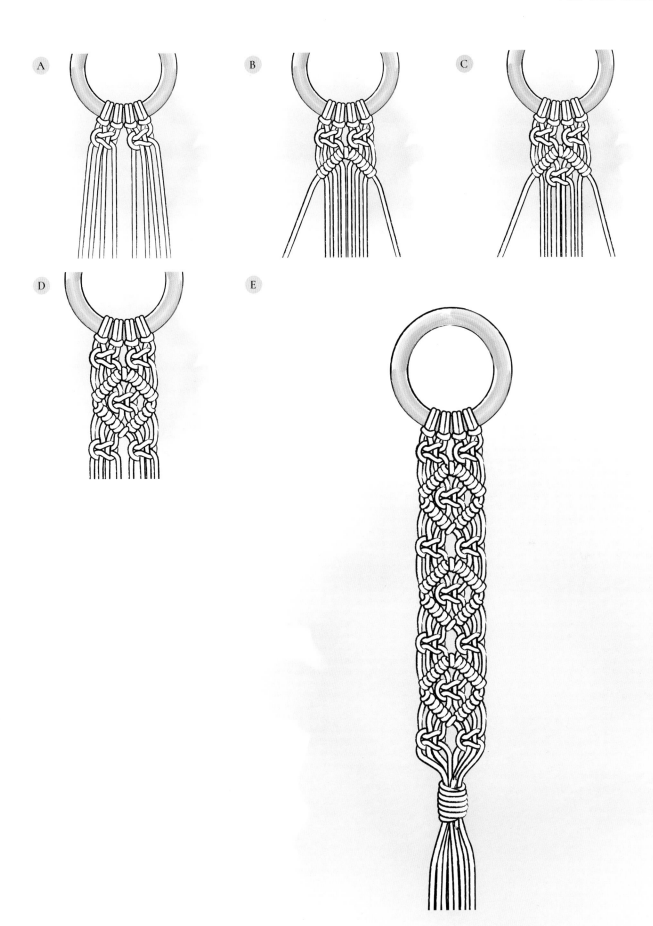

FISHTAIL CHAIN

This distinctively shaped diamond chain is formed by working rows of diagonal double half hitch knots beneath each other, starting from the centre out and decreasing the number of knots tied on each row.

MATERIALS

- Four 175cm (69in) lengths of 3mm (⅛in) macramé cord
- One 80cm (32in) length of 3mm (⅛in) macramé cord
- 5.5cm (2¼in) wooden ring

FINISHED SIZE

Width: 6cm (2⅜in)

Length: 33cm (13in)

1. Take the four 175cm (69in) cord lengths, fold them in half and attach them onto the wooden ring using forward lark's head knots (see Single-Strand Knots), to give you eight working cords.

2. Join the middle two cords using a half knot (see Square Knots); these will become the static cords that the diagonal double half hitches will be tied onto (A).

3. Starting from the centre and working diagonally outwards to the left, take the left-hand static cord and tie three diagonal double half hitches onto it with the three left-hand hanging cords (see Half Hitch Knots) (B). Now mirror the actions on the right-hand side, taking the right-hand static cord and tying three diagonal double half hitches onto it with the three right-hand hanging cords (C).

4. For the second row, again start by joining the middle cords with a half knot. Using the cords of the half knot as your static cords, tie diagonal double half hitches onto them from the centre out, first to the left and then to the right, but this time using only the first two hanging cords on each side (D, E).

5. For the third row, join the middle two cords with a half knot as before, but this time tie only one diagonal double half hitch to each side.

6. For the final row, using the middle cords, choose one cord to be the static cord and tie one diagonal double half hitch with the other cord (if you are right-hand dominant, it is most likely that it will be more comfortable to use the left-hand cord as the static cord, and vice versa). The first diamond is now complete (F).

7. Leaving a small space of approx. 1cm (⅜in), join the two middle cords with a half knot and repeat steps 3 to 6 to make another diamond (G).

8. Continue to make diamonds until you have four in total. To finish, bundle the working cords together and fasten with a wrap knot made from the remaining 80cm (32in) length of cord (see Single-Strand Knots), trimming the ends to be the same length (H).

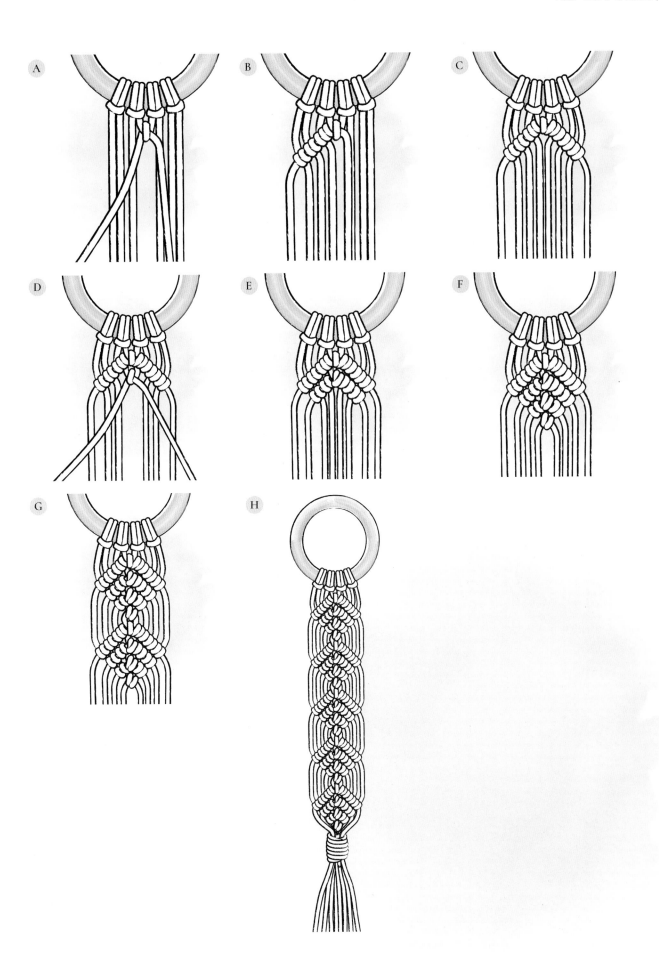

SIX-CORD CHAINS

Six-cord chains have more working cords than four-cord chains and this enables even more interesting shapes to be created from basic knot combinations. Each of the three featured designs teach a shape and knot combination and then repeat it, further building on your understanding of how macramé patterns are formed, and taking you one step further to creating your own wall hanging designs. Each chain begins in the same way, by tying six lengths of cord onto a small wooden dowel using forward lark's head knots to give you twelve working cords.

DIAGONAL DHH DIAMOND CHAIN WITH ALTERNATING SQUARE KNOTS

A popular choice for macramé wall hanging patterns, this six-cord variation of a diamond chain combines diagonal double half hitch (dhh) and square knots to make a more complex and eye-catching diamond motif than that seen in the four-cord diamond chains.

MATERIALS

- Six 230cm (91in) lengths of 4mm (⁵⁄₃₂in) macramé cord
- Two 60cm (24in) lengths of 4mm (⁵⁄₃₂in) macramé cord
- One 80cm (32in) length of 4mm (⁵⁄₃₂in) macramé cord
- 12cm (5in) length of 18mm (⁵⁄₈in) wooden dowel

FINISHED SIZE

Width: 10cm (4in)

Length: 50cm (20in)

1. Take the six 230cm (91in) cord lengths, fold each in half and attach them onto the wooden dowel using forward lark's head knots (see Single-Strand Knots), to give you twelve working cords. Also using forward lark's head knots, attach the 60cm (24in) cord lengths at either end of the dowel, turn them so the knots sit behind the dowel, then join the ends with an overhand knot (see Single-Strand Knots) to create a hanging loop (A).

2. Take the middle two cords and join them together using a half knot (see Square Knots); these will become the static cords that the diagonal double half hitches will be tied onto (B).

A

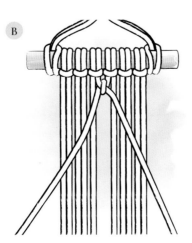

B

3. Working from the centre to the left, place the left-hand static cord diagonally and tie five diagonal double half hitches onto it with the left-hand hanging cords (see Half Hitch Knots) (C).

4. Then, mirroring your actions, take the right-hand static cord and tie five diagonal double half hitches onto it with the right-hand hanging cords (D).

5. For the next row, repeat steps 2 to 4 to tie another row of diagonal double half hitches to each side (E).

6. Identity the middle four cords and tie a left facing square knot (see Square Knots) (F).

7. Directly below, separate the working cords of the square knot to identify the two left-hand cords. Taking these together with the two hanging cords to the left, tie the first of two square knots on this row. Identifying the two right-hand cords from the square knot above and taking these together with the two hanging cords to the right, tie the second square knot in an alternating square knot pattern (G).

8. Directly below, identify the middle four cords once more and tie a square knot to complete the alternating square knot pattern (H).

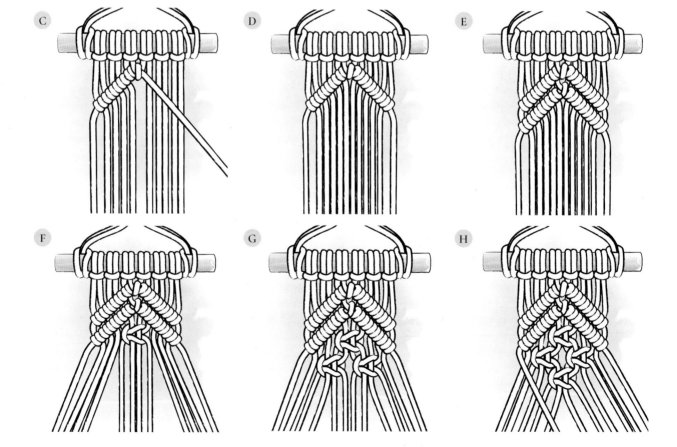

9. Continuing to form the diamond motif, take the far left-hand cord and place it diagonally into the centre. This becomes the static cord onto which five diagonal double half hitches will be tied with the hanging cords, working from the left to the middle. Mirror your actions on the right-hand side, bringing the far right-hand cord diagonally into the centre, and working from the right to the middle to tie five diagonal double half hitches with the hanging cords. Join the static cords in the middle using a half knot (I, J, K).

10. Repeat step 9 to work the second row of diagonal double half hitches to complete the first half of the chain (L).

11. Repeat steps 2 to 10 to tie a second diamond motif.

12. To finish, bundle the working cords together and fasten with a wrap knot made from the remaining 80cm (32in) length of cord (see Single-Strand Knots), trimming the ends to be the same length (M).

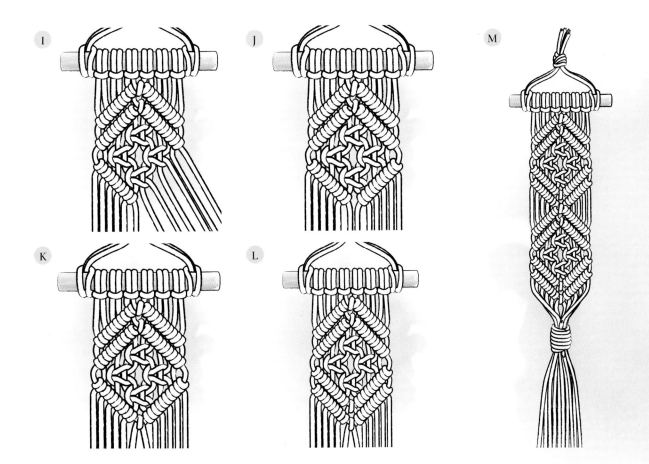

BUTTERFLY CHAIN

This butterfly chain starts by creating rows of diagonal double half hitches from the outside inwards, working a second row to each side before joining at the centre with a square knot. The X-shape motif is then completed by working diagonal double half hitch rows from the centre outwards, and when repeated, a diamond shape emerges. This motif is useful for making longer items, such as macramé belts or curtain tie backs.

MATERIALS

- Six 280cm (110in) lengths of 4mm (⁵⁄₃₂in) macramé cord
- Two 60cm (24in) lengths of 4mm (⁵⁄₃₂in) macramé cord
- One 80cm (32in) length of 4mm (⁵⁄₃₂in) macramé cord
- 12cm (5in) length of 18mm (⁵⁄₈in) wooden dowel

FINISHED SIZE

Width: 8cm (3⅛in)

Length: 62cm (24½in)

1. Take the six 280cm (110in) cord lengths, fold each in half and attach them onto the wooden dowel using forward lark's head knots (see Single-Strand Knots), to give you twelve working cords. Also using forward lark's head knots, attach the 60cm (24in) cord lengths at either end of the dowel, turn them so the knots sit behind the dowel, then join the ends with an overhand knot (see Single-Strand Knots) to create a hanging loop. Separate the hanging cords in half.

2. Starting with the left-hand set of six hanging cords, place the first cord diagonally into the centre to become the static cord and tie five diagonal double half hitches (see Half Hitch Knots) onto it with the left-hand hanging cords, working towards the centre (A).

3. Then, mirroring your actions on the right-hand set of six hanging cords, place the last cord diagonally into the centre to become the static cord and tie five diagonal double half hitches onto it with the right-hand hanging cords, working in towards the centre (B).

4. Repeat steps 2 and 3 to tie another row of diagonal double half hitches directly below the first (C, D, E).

5. To join the rows of diagonal double half hitches on each side to form the top of the X-shape, take the middle four cords and tie a square knot (see Square Knots) (F).

6. To create the bottom of the X-shape, work rows of diagonal double half hitch from the centre outwards. First identify the middle two cords and split them to the left and the right. These will be the static cords for the diagonal double half hitch rows. Working on the left-hand static cord first, tie five diagonal double half hitches from the middle outwards. Then, mirroring your actions on the right-hand static cord, tie five diagonal double half hitches from the middle outwards (G).

7. Repeat step 6 to work a second row of diagonal double half hitches to each side to complete the X-shaped butterfly motif (H).

8. Repeat steps 2 to 7 twice more to complete a chain of three motifs.

9. To finish, bundle the working cords together and fasten with a wrap knot made from the remaining 80cm (32in) length of cord (see Single-Strand Knots), trimming the ends to be the same length (I).

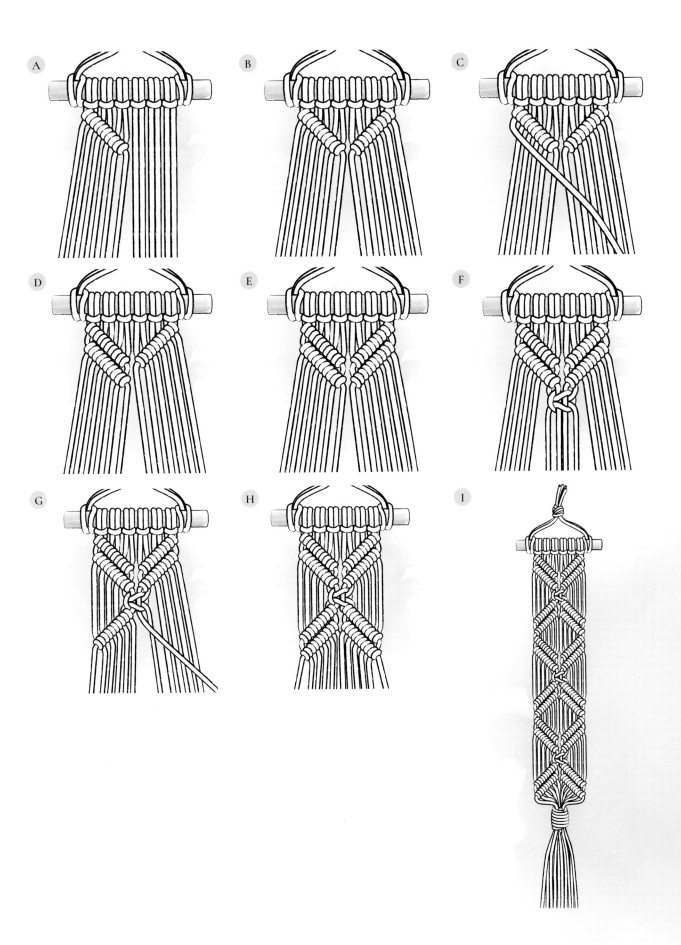

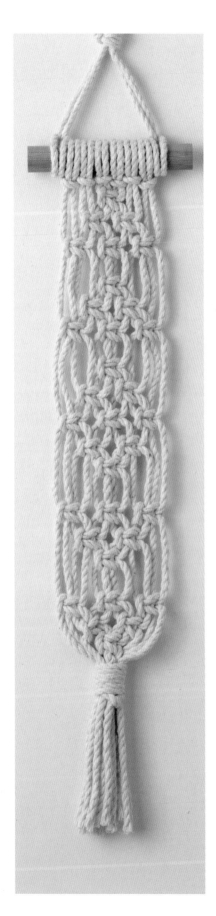

TRIANGLES AND DIAMONDS CHAIN

This chain offers the chance to practise the alternating square knot technique to make an upward-pointing triangle and a downward-pointing triangle, which when combined create a diamond motif. Choose your square knot preference, left or right facing (see Square Knots), and ensure you tie all the knots this way.

MATERIALS

- Six 240cm (94½in) lengths of 4mm (⁵⁄₃₂in) macramé cord
- Two 60cm (24in) lengths of 4mm (⁵⁄₃₂in) macramé cord
- One 80cm (32in) length of 4mm (⁵⁄₃₂in) macramé cord
- 12cm (5in) length of 18mm (⅝in) wooden dowel

FINISHED SIZE

Width: 8cm (3⅛in)

Length: 62cm (24½in)

1. Take the six 240cm (94½in) cord lengths, fold each in half and attach them onto the wooden dowel using forward lark's head knots (see Single-Strand Knots), to give you twelve working cords. Also using forward lark's head knots, attach the 60cm (24in) cord lengths at either end of the dowel, turn them so the knots sit behind the dowel, then join the ends with an overhand knot (see Single-Strand Knots) to create a hanging loop.

2. The first motif in the chain is an upward-pointing triangle, made by alternating cords across three rows of square knots in an increasing pattern. Start by identifying the middle four cords (cords 5 to 8) and tie a square knot to complete row 1.

3. On row 2, tie two square knots using cords 3 to 6 and cords 7 to 10.

4. On row 3, tie three square knots using cords 1 to 4, cords 5 to 8 and cords 9 to 12. This completes the first of the upward-pointing triangles (A).

5. Leave a space of approximately a row's width, then repeat steps 2 to 4 to create another upward-pointing triangle (B).

6. The motif in the middle of the chain is a diamond, made by alternating cords across five rows of square knots in an increasing/ decreasing pattern. Allowing for a space of a row's width, start by repeating steps 2 to 4 to create an upward-pointing triangle (rows 1 to 3). On row 4, tie two square knots using cords 3 to 6 and cords 7 to 10 (C). On row 5, tie one square knot using cords 5 to 8 to complete the diamond motif.

7. The next motif in the chain is a downward-pointing triangle, made by alternating cords across three rows of square knots in a decreasing pattern as shown in diagrams D-F. Allowing for a space of a row's width, start by tying a row of three square knots from left to right using all cords (D). On row 2, tie two square knots using cords 3 to 6 and cords 7 to 10 (E), and on row 3, tie just one square knot using cords 5 to 8 (F).

8. Leave a space of approximately a row's width, then repeat step 7 to create another downward-pointing triangle.

9. To finish, bundle the working cords together and fasten with a wrap knot made from the remaining 80cm (32in) length of cord (see Single-Strand Knots), trimming the ends to be the same length (G).

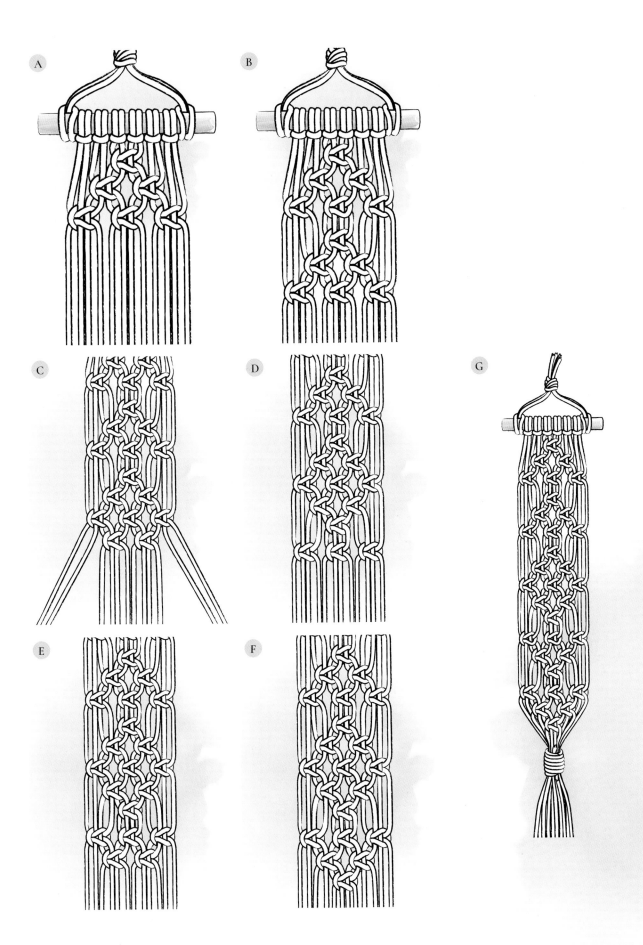

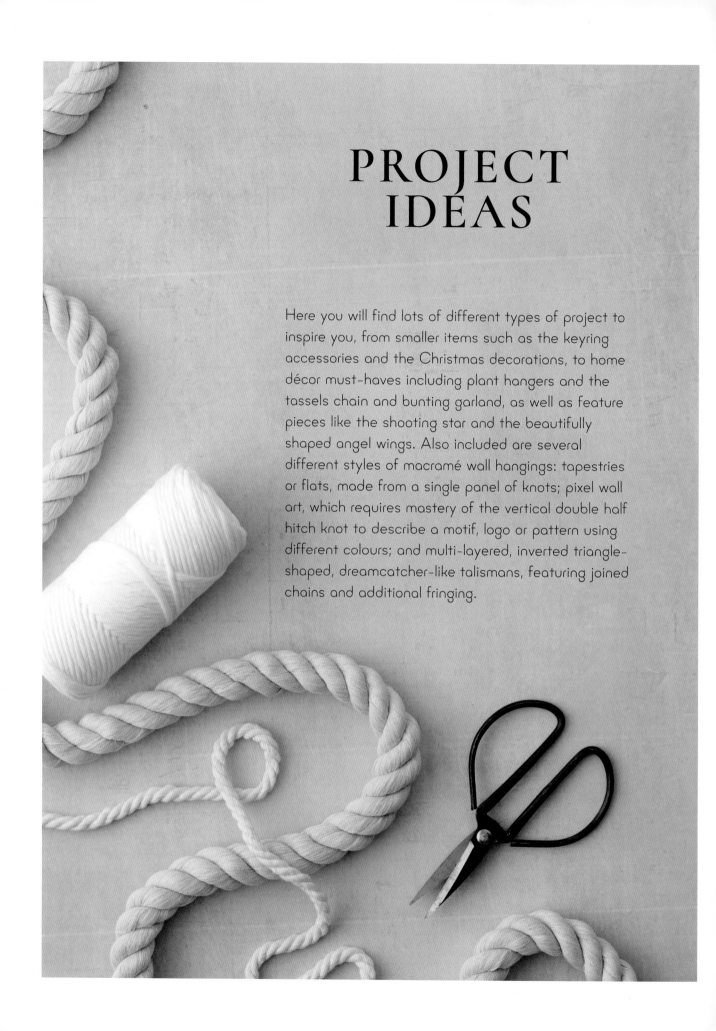

PROJECT IDEAS

Here you will find lots of different types of project to inspire you, from smaller items such as the keyring accessories and the Christmas decorations, to home décor must-haves including plant hangers and the tassels chain and bunting garland, as well as feature pieces like the shooting star and the beautifully shaped angel wings. Also included are several different styles of macramé wall hangings: tapestries or flats, made from a single panel of knots; pixel wall art, which requires mastery of the vertical double half hitch knot to describe a motif, logo or pattern using different colours; and multi-layered, inverted triangle-shaped, dreamcatcher-like talismans, featuring joined chains and additional fringing.

KEYRING
ACCESSORIES

These are a joy to give as gifts and quick to make, and there are two styles to choose from. The pretty yet functional wristlet is made by repeating square knots, one after the other. The fishtail design of the mermaid tail, created using a diagonal double half hitch knot pattern, features a decorative bead accent. Both are easy to personalize – express yourself in your choice of keyring finding and cord colours.

MATERIALS

Wristlet Keyring
- 5.4m (18¼ft) of 3mm (⅛in) 3-ply or single-ply macramé cord

Mermaid Tail Keyring
- 4.4m (14½ft) of 3mm (⅛in) 3-ply or single-ply macramé cord
- 1 x small wooden bead

For Both Keyrings
- Lobster clasp keyring finding

FINISHED SIZE

Wristlet Keyring
Width: 2cm (¾in)
Length: 20cm (8in)

Mermaid Tail Keyring
Width: 4cm (1½in)
Length: 24cm (9½in)

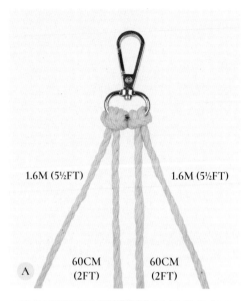

1.6M (5½FT)   1.6M (5½FT)

60CM (2FT)   60CM (2FT)

A

B

C

PATTERN NOTES

When making the wristlet keyring all the square knots must be tied in the same way, either all left facing or all right facing, so pick your orientation and stick with it. The samples are made using left facing square knots.

Once the wristlet keyring is complete, you might want to add a drop of fabric glue beneath the loops of the wrap knot for extra security.

PREPARATION FOR WRISTLET KEYRING

- Cut 2 x 2.2m (7½ft) lengths of cord
- Cut 1 x 1m (3¼ft) length of cord

KNOTS

- Forward Lark's Head Knot
- Square Knot
- Wrap Knot

METHOD FOR WRISTLET KEYRING

1. Take each 2.2m (7½ft) length of cord and fold to measure 1.6m (5½ft) on one side and 60cm (2ft) on the other. Attach cords to the lobster clasp keyring finding with forward lark's head knots (see Single-Strand Knots), making sure that the longer lengths are on the outside and the shorter lengths are on the inside (A).

2. Tie a square knot tight to the keyring finding. Leave a 2cm (¾in) space then tie another square knot (B).

3. Tie a sinnet (vertical column) of about twenty-six square knots, stopping when you have approx. 10cm (4in) of length remaining on your working cords.

4. Bring the ends of the working cords up to pass them through the hoop at the base of the lobster clasp, resting them to one side of the square knot sinnet, alongside the space left in step 2 (C).

5. Using the 1m (3¼ft) length of cord, tie a wrap knot with nine wraps or more (see Single-Strand Knots) around the top of the wristlet, to secure the cord lengths folded over the keyring finding. Trim off any excess cord from the wrap knot.

PATTERN NOTES

When making the mermaid tail keyring ensure the cord you are using will thread through the hole in the accent bead you choose.

It's advisable to make this design with a single-ply cord if you want to achieve the 'flipper tail' fringing.

PREPARATION FOR MERMAID TAIL KEYRING

- Cut 3 x 1.3m (51¼in) lengths of cord
- Cut 1 x 50cm (20in) length of cord

KNOTS

- Reverse Lark's Head Knot
- Diagonal Double Half Hitches
- Half Knot
- Wrap Knot

METHOD FOR MERMAID TAIL KEYRING

1. Attach the three 1.3m (51¼in) lengths of cord to the lobster clasp keyring finding with reverse lark's head knots (see Single-Strand Knots), to give you six working cords.

2. Identify the middle two cords (cords 3 and 4) and thread them through the small wooden bead.

3. Bring the left-hand cord (cord 1) down diagonally towards the middle to become a static cord and tie diagonal double half hitches onto it using cords 2 and 3 (see Half Hitch Knots), finishing as close to the base of the bead as possible.

4. Mirroring step 3 on the right-hand side, bring the right-hand cord (cord 6) down diagonally towards the middle to become a static cord and tie diagonal double half hitches onto it using cords 5 and 4.

5. Join the static cords using a half knot (see Square Knots).

6 Repeat steps 3 to 5 to tie eight more rows of diagonal double half hitches from the outside in towards to the middle.

7. Bundle the remaining working cords together and secure using the 50cm (20in) cord length to tie a wrap knot with five wraps (see Single-Strand Knots). Trim off any excess cord from the wrap knot.

8. Use a pet hairbrush to brush out the cords to create the 'flipper' of the mermaid tail.

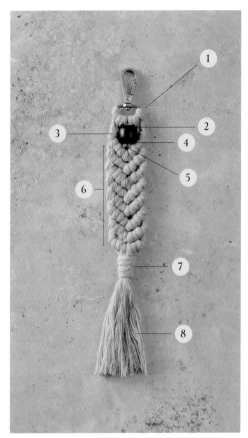

PLANT HANGERS

DIFFICULTY

MATERIALS

For Each Plant Hanger

- 25.7m (84½ft) of 4mm (⁵⁄₃₂in) macramé cord in main colour
- 1.2m (4ft) of 4mm (⁵⁄₃₂in) macramé cord in accent colour

FINISHED SIZE

Width: 4cm (1½in)
Length: 91cm (3ft)

PREPARATION

For Each Plant Hanger

- Cut 1 x 2.3m (7¾ft) length of cord in main colour
- Cut 6 x 3.9m (12¾ft) lengths of cord in main colour
- Cut 2 x 60cm (24in) lengths of cord in accent colour

KNOTS

- Wrap Knot
- Wrap Knot Hanging Loop
- Square Knot
- Half Knot Spiral
- Alternating Square Knots

Plant hangers are one of the most popular macramé homeware accessories and they come in so many different styles. These two designs feature just two of the most popular knots – the square knot sinnet and the half knot spiral – creating the 'arms' of the plant hanger. Flipping the order in which the knots are tied creates an alternative look to make a complementary pair.

PATTERN NOTES

These two projects demonstrate the most popular style of plant hanger, formed from a wrap knot hanging loop at the top, with three 'arms' made from macramé knot sinnets, and a basket shape at the bottom to hold a pot, secured in place with a wrap knot tassel to finish.

Once the wrap knot hanging loop has been tied, attach it to an S-hook and hang this from a clothes rail to work the long hanging cords vertically.

Work on the arms one at a time, then join them to make the basket. One key point to remember when working the pattern for the arms is that, when moving from one style of sinnet to the other, it is important to switch the outside working cords of the previous sinnet to be the middle static cords of the next sinnet.

Using an accent colour for the wrap knots gives this classic design a contemporary vibe.

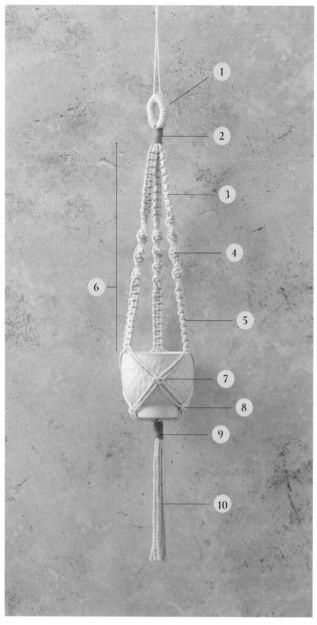

METHOD FOR PLANT HANGER 1

1. Referring to the Wrap Knot Hanging Loop technique (see Single-Strand Knots), bunch the six 3.9m (12¾ft) lengths of cord together and use the 2.3m (7¾ft) length of same colour cord to tie a wrap knot at the midway point (thirty-six wraps).

2. Fold the main colour cord wrap knot in half and tie a second wrap knot at its base with a 60cm (2ft) length of accent cord (nine wraps).

3. Separate the cords into three groups of four cords ready to make the arms of the plant hanger. Working with the first group of four cords, tie ten square knots (see Square Knots) in a sinnet (vertical column).

4. Switching the outside working cords to be the middle static cords (A), tie twenty half knots in a sinnet to form a half knot spiral (see Square Knots).

5. Again switching the outside working cords to be the middle static cords, tie ten square knots in a sinnet to complete the first arm.

6. Repeat steps 3 to 5 with the remaining two groups of four cords to make two more arms.

7. Now start to make the basket. Leave a space of 8cm (3⅛in), then tie a row of alternating square knots (see Square Knots) to join the arms: take two cords from neighbouring square knots to tie each square knot, tying a total of three square knots in the row.

8. Leave a space of 8cm (3⅛in), then tie another row of three alternating square knots below the previous row.

9. Leave a space of 8cm (3⅛in) and, to form the bottom of the basket, tie a wrap knot around all the working cords with the remaining 60cm (2ft) length of accent cord (nine wraps).

10. Trim the tassel cords to your desired length.

METHOD FOR PLANT HANGER 2

1. Repeat step 1 of Plant Hanger 1.

2. Repeat step 2 of Plant Hanger 1.

3. Separate the cords into three groups of four cords ready to make the arms of the plant hanger. Working with the first group of four cords, tie twenty half knots in a sinnet to form a half knot spiral (see Square Knots).

4. Switching the outside working cords to be the middle static cords (B), tie ten square knots (see Square Knots) in a sinnet (vertical column).

5. Again switching the outside working cords to be the middle static cords, tie twenty half knots in a sinnet to form a half knot spiral, to complete the first arm.

6. Repeat steps 3 to 5 with the remaining two groups of four cords to make two more arms.

7. Repeat step 7 of Plant Hanger 1.

8. Repeat step 8 of Plant Hanger 1.

9. Repeat step 9 of Plant Hanger 1.

10. Repeat step 10 of Plant Hanger 1.

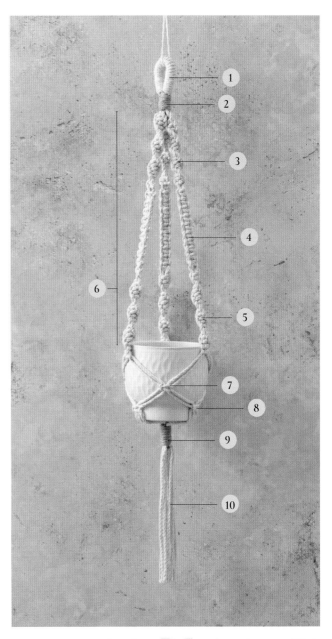

FEATHERS
AND LEAVES

DIFFICULTY

MATERIALS

Feather

- 3.8m (12¾ft) of 3mm (⅛in) macramé cord in main colour
- 4m (13½ft) of 3mm (⅛in) macramé cord in contrasting colour

Leaf

- 15.7m (52ft) of 3mm (⅛in) macramé cord
- 12cm (4¾in) length of 2cm (¾in) wooden dowel

For Both

- Self-adhesive felt
- Fabric stiffener (optional)

FINISHED SIZE

Width: 19cm (7½in)
Length: 25cm (9⅞in)

Feathers and leaves are quick, easy-to-make projects, ideal for creating on your table top. Requiring only small amounts of cord, they are a good way to use up leftover lengths from other projects. Start with the feather pattern if you are a beginner, then move on to the leaf design, which is tied with a repeating knot pattern of diagonal double half hitches directed from the centre outwards, just like the veins on leaves!

PATTERN NOTES

Both designs, and the feather in particular, gain impact from the brushing out of the fringing and, to get the best results, it is important to use single-ply cords.

A template has been provided to help you achieve the distinctive outline of both designs (see Template).

The feather design has a felt backing to help maintain its shape, but some artists like to use fabric stiffener or glue (or sometimes even hairspray) to further fix the fibres of the leaf. In fact, sometimes I use only fabric stiffener (Mod Podge Stiffy) instead of a felt backing. Do experiment to see what your preference is.

PREPARATION FOR FEATHER

- Cut 1 x 60cm (24in) length of cord in main colour
- Cut 8 x 40cm (16in) lengths of cord in main colour
- Cut 10 x 40cm (16in) lengths of cord in contrasting colour

KNOTS

- Overhand Knot
- Reverse Lark's Head Knot
- Half Knot

METHOD FOR FEATHER

1. Take the 60cm (24in) length of your main colour cord (white), fold it in half and close to the fold tie an overhand knot (see Single-Strand Knots) to leave a small loop for hanging. This now becomes the shaft of the feather, forming the foundation cords onto which your fringing cords are tied.

2. Starting with a length of 40cm (16in) cord of the contrasting colour (brown), fold it in half and, working from the left-hand side, attach it to the foundation cords with a reverse lark's head knot (see Single-Strand Knots). Make sure to tie it directly beneath the knot above (A).

3. Take another length of 40cm (16in) cord again in your contrasting colour, fold it in half and attach it to the foundation cords with a reverse lark's head knot, this time working from the right-hand side and again making sure to tie it directly beneath the knot above (A).

4. Repeat steps 2 and 3 to attach the remaining 40cm (16in) lengths of contrasting colour cord, alternating the direction each time (ten cords in total).

5. Following the method described in steps 2 to 4, attach the eight 40cm (16in) lengths of main colour cord to the foundation cords using reverse lark's heads knots and remembering to alternate the direction of the cords each time.

6. Once all the fringing cords have been attached to the foundation cords, tie the ends of the foundation cords with a half knot to secure (see Square Knots).

7. Brush out the fringing cords, starting from the ends (B). Use a softer brush to begin with, and once nearly untwisted use a finer brush to remove the fibre fluff and continue to flatten out until quite smooth (this takes about 5–10 minutes depending on the cord being used).

8. Use the feather/leaf template (see Template) to cut a piece of self-adhesive felt to make a backing for your finished feather decoration.

9. Turn the feather over to the wrong side and brush it out to your desired shape, making sure that there are no gaps where your fringed cord is laying. Peel off the self-adhesive felt and place it centrally over your feather (C).

10. Flip the feather back over to the right side and brush gently to embed the fibres into the self-adhesive felt. Once you are happy with the arrangement, place the feather onto a cutting mat ready to trim the cords to the final shape. Using a rotary cutter, start from the bottom and cut upwards in a curve to the top on each side (D).

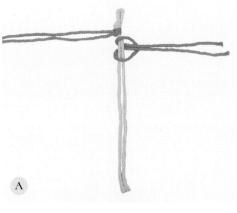

A

B

C

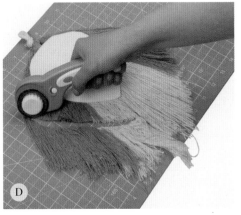

D

PREPARATION FOR LEAF

- Cut 6 x 1.6m (5¼ft) lengths of cord
- Cut 1 x 50cm (20in) length of cord
- Cut 14 x 40cm (16in) lengths of cord

KNOTS

- Forward Lark's Head Knot
- Reverse Lark's Head Knot
- Overhand Knot
- Diagonal Double Half Hitches

METHOD FOR LEAF

1. Take the 50cm (20in) length of cord, fold it in half and attach it to the middle of the dowel using a forward lark's head knot (see Single-Strand Knots). Join the ends using an overhand knot (see Single-Strand Knots) to create a hanging loop.

2. Turn the dowel so that the hanging loop is at the top. Now attach three 1.6m (5¼ft) lengths of cord to either side of the hanging loop, again using forward lark's head knots, to give you twelve working cords.

3. Create the large fishtail diamond using all twelve hanging cords, as follows:

Row 1: Join the middle two cords using a half knot (see Square Knots); these will become the static cords that the diagonal double half hitches will be tied onto. Starting from the centre and working diagonally outwards to the left, take the left-hand static cord and tie five diagonal double half hitches onto it with the five left-hand hanging cords (see Half Hitch Knots). Now mirror the actions on the right-hand side, taking the right-hand static cord and tying five diagonal double half hitches onto it with the five right-hand hanging cords.

Row 2: As Row 1 but tying four diagonal double half hitches on each side.

Row 3: As Row 1 but tying three diagonal double half hitches on each side.

Row 4: As Row 1 but tying two diagonal double half hitches on each side.

Row 5: As Row 1 but tying one diagonal double half hitch on the right-hand side only.

Row 6: For the final row, using the middle cords, choose one cord to be the static cord and tie one diagonal double half hitch with the other cord either to the left or the right, depending on whether you are right-hand or left-hand dominant.

4. Leave a small space then create the small fishtail diamond on the central eight hanging cords only (see steps 2 to 7 of the Fishtail Chain in Four-Cord Chains for detailed instruction for making the small fishtail diamond motif) (A).

5. Add the additional fringing cords above the large fishtail diamond motif. Take a 40cm (16in) length of cord and attach it using the reverse lark's head knot onto the first pair of cords on the left-hand side (B). Repeat to attach two more cord lengths.

6. Add the additional fringing cords between the large and small fishtail diamond motifs. Attach four 40cm (16in) lengths of cord using the reverse lark's head knot onto the outer cord that joins the diamond motifs on the left-hand side (C).

7. Repeat steps 5 and 6 on the right-hand side using the remaining seven 40cm (16in) lengths of cord.

8. Brush out the fringing cords using a pet hairbrush. Placing your brushed out project onto a cutting mat, use a rotary cutter to cut the fringe into a leaf shape using the feather/leaf template as a guide (see Template).

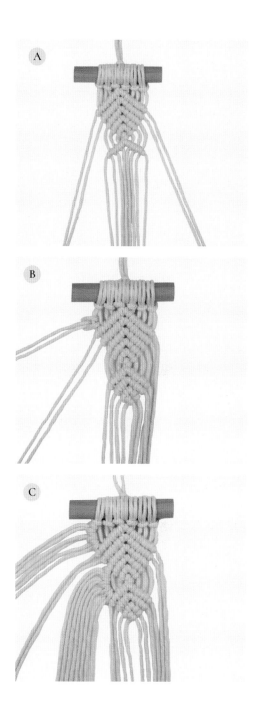

BUNTING GARLAND

MATERIALS
- 23.6m (77½ft) of 4mm (⁵⁄₃₂in) macramé cord

FINISHED SIZE

Each Flag
Width: 18cm (7in)
Length: 29cm (11⅜in)

PREPARATION

Foundation Cord
- Cut 1 x 2m (6½ft) length of cord

Each Flag
- Cut 12 x 1.6m (5¼ft) lengths of cord
- Cut 6 x 40cm (16in) lengths of cord

KNOTS
- Forward Lark's Head Knot
- Alternating Square Knots
- Diagonal Double Half Hitches
- Half Knot
- Rya Tassels

Bunting always has a celebratory feel to it, making it a favourite for makers of macramé everywhere. This design is made onto a foundation cord, and once you have mastered the tying of a single bunting flag, you can make as many as you choose for a garland that meets your decorating needs.

PATTERN NOTES

Materials given are for making a garland of five bunting flags, i.e. 12 x 1.6m (5¼ft) lengths of cord for each bunting flag. If you want to make your garland longer or shorter, simply adjust your overall cord requirements.

METHOD

1. Take the foundation cord and lay it out horizontally onto your work surface. Find the middle of the cord and place a piece of masking tape 15cm (6in) to each side of the centre point, to secure it to your table top. This marks the area where the central bunting flag will be tied.

2. Take the twelve 1.6m (5¼ft) lengths of cord, fold each in half and attach them to the foundation cord (i.e. in the middle of the marked space) using forward lark's head knots (see Single-Strand Knots), to give you twenty-four working cords.

3. Identify the middle four cords (cords 11 to 14) and tie a square knot (see Square Knots). Tie two square knots to either side of the first square knot, leaving two cords untied at each side. This completes the first row.

4. Starting at the left-hand edge, tie a square knot with cords 1 to 4, and continue to tie square knots across the row, alternating cords with the row above, to tie a total of six square knots to complete the second row.

5. On the third row, identify the middle four cords (cords 11 to 14) and leave these untied, tying two square knots to either side. This gives you a row of four square knots with two untied cords at each side.

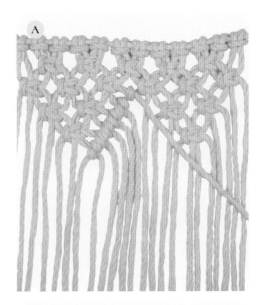

6. For the fourth and final row of the alternating square knot pattern, alternate cords from the square knots tied in the third row to tie a row of two square knots.

7. Returning to the untied cords at the base of the second row, identify the two middle cords (cords 12 and 13) and tie together with a half knot (see Square Knots). Bring the left-hand cord down diagonally to the left, to be a static cord on which to tie five diagonal double half hitches (see Half Hitch Knots) with the five hanging cords to the left, leaving six cords untied at the left-hand edge (A).

8. Then, mirroring your actions on the right-hand side, bring the right-hand cord down diagonally to the right, to be a static cord on which to tie five diagonal double half hitches with the five hanging cords to the right, leaving six cords untied at the right-hand edge.

9. Bring cord 1 down diagonally to the centre, to be a static cord on which to tie diagonal half hitch knots with cords 2 to 12.

10. Mirroring your actions on the right-hand side, bring cord 24 down diagonally to the centre, to be a static cord on which to tie diagonal half hitch knots with cords 23 to 13. Join the two rows of diagonal half hitches together in the middle with a half knot (B).

11. Repeat steps 9 and 10 to complete the second row of diagonal double half hitch knots that defines the pennant shape.

12. To fill the diamond shape, use the six 40cm (16in) lengths of cord to tie a rya tassel (see Four-Cord Chains: Rya Tassels).

13. Repeat steps 2 to 12 to make four more flags, two to either side of the middle flag, approximately 5cm (2in) apart.

14. Once all five flags are complete, work on a cutting board using a rotary cutter to cut the fringe to shape – I like to keep my middle section a little longer, approximately 15cm (6in) at the tip of the point.

— ANGEL WINGS —

MATERIALS
- 101m (336¾ft) of 3mm (⅛in) single ply macramé cord
- 50cm (20in) length of 20mm (¾in) wooden dowel

FINISHED SIZE
Width: 50cm (20in)
Length: 65cm (26in)

PREPARATION
- Cut 1 x 3.4m (11¼ft) length of cord
- Cut 24 x 2.4m (8ft) lengths of cord
- Cut 50 x 80cm (32in) lengths of cord

KNOTS
- Forward Lark's Head
- Horizontal Double Half Hitches
- Diagonal Double Half Hitches
- Square Knot
- Alternating Square Knots

This sweet wall hanging is perfect for nursery decor. It requires you to know just two basic knot principles, how to tie double half hitch knots and alternating square knots under the correct tension to get the right curvy shapes and diagonal angles to create the 'feathers' in these wings.

PATTERN NOTES

This pattern is symmetrical. The step instructions are given working across each wing in turn at each stage of the tying process, first on the left side, then on the right, which is how I like to work. However, if you prefer, you can create one complete wing before moving on to tie the other, trying your best to make them match!

To achieve the distinctive curved shape at the top of each wing, which is a key feature of this pattern, first a long foundation cord is attached to the dowel, then the working cords are attached to this foundation cord using the looping lark's head technique (see Getting Started). Achieving a good shape to begin with is important as this becomes your guide for the shaping of the double half hitch rows that follow.

Although this pattern requires only basic knots, the challenge is to tie them under the correct tension and to ensure that they are well placed for perfect symmetry across the wings.

It is recommended that you hang the dowel from a clothes rail using S-hooks to work vertically when making this project.

METHOD

1. Fold the 3.4m (11¼ft) length of cord in half and attach it the centre of the dowel using the looping lark's head technique (see Getting Started), tying the side knots about 8cm (3⅛in) from the ends of the dowel. This is the foundation cord onto which all the working cords will be tied (A).

2. Take twelve of the 2.4m (8ft) lengths of cord and, folding each in half, attach them onto the foundation cord to the left-hand side of the central knot; these are the working cords for the left-hand wing. Attach the remaining twelve lengths of 2.4m (8ft) cord to the right-hand side of the central knot in the same way; these are the working cords for the right-hand wing.

3. Once all the working cords have been attached, you need to pull on the foundation cord lengths at either side to adjust the size of the loops that the working cords are hanging on, tightening up the space to create the right shape. The cords should be relaxed when hanging, fitting nicely together without bunching up (B). Ensure each side matches the other (you might want to measure to be sure).

4. Working on the left-hand wing first, tie a row of horizontal double half hitch knots (see Half Hitch Knots) with the left-hand set of working cords. Make the right-hand cord of the set your static cord, and working from the centre out to the left-hand edge, tie double half hitch knots onto it with each of the hanging cords, including the hanging foundation cord at the left-hand edge, placing your knots to match the curved shape already established.

5. Now working on the right-hand wing, tie a row of horizontal double half hitch knots with the right-hand set of working cords. Make the left-hand cord of the set your static cord, and working from the centre out to the right-hand edge, tie double half hitch knots onto it with each of the hanging cords, including the hanging foundation cord at the right-hand edge, placing your knots to match the curved shape already established.

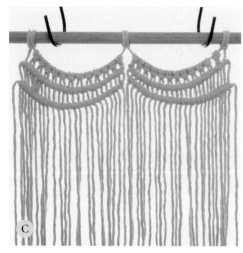

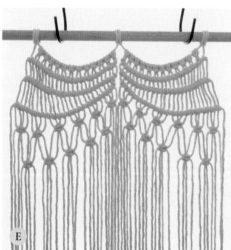

6. Returning to the left-hand wing, repeat step 4 to tie a second row of double half hitch knots from the centre outwards, paying particular attention to the tensioning of the static cord and the placing of the knots to achieve the shaping of the row. Start by keeping the first four or five knots close to the previous row but slightly diagonal, then work with a more horizontal orientation, ensuring that the space between the two rows of knots is increasing as you work towards the outer edge, but that the curved shape is maintained (C).

7. Moving over to the right-hand wing, repeat step 5 to tie a second row of double half hitch knots from the centre outwards, paying particular attention to match the shaping of the same row of double half hitch knots on the left-hand wing, as detailed in step 6 (C).

8. Returning to the left-hand wing, repeat step 6 to tie a third row of double half hitch knots from the centre outwards (D).

9. Moving over to the right-hand wing, repeat step 7 to tie a third row of double half hitch knots from the centre outwards, paying particular attention to match the shaping of the same row of double half hitch knots on the left-hand wing (D).

10. Returning to the left-hand wing, tie a row of six square knots (see Square Knots) in a diagonal orientation, working from the centre outwards, to leave a single hanging cord unworked at the left-hand edge.

11. Moving over to the right-hand wing, tie a row of six square knots in a diagonal orientation, working from the centre outwards, to leave a single hanging cord unworked at the right-hand edge. Pay particular attention to make sure that the placing of the square knots on the right-hand wing is in alignment with those on the left-hand wing.

12. Returning to the left-hand wing, tie a row of five square knots in an alternating square knot pattern (see Square Knots), again in a diagonal orientation, working from the centre outwards. This will leave three hanging cords unworked at the left-hand edge (E).

13. Moving over to the right-hand wing, tie a row of five square knots in an alternating square knot pattern, again in a diagonal orientation, working from the centre outwards. This will leave three hanging cords unworked at the right-hand edge (E). Pay particular attention to make sure that the placing of the square knots on the right-hand wing is in alignment with those on the left-hand wing.

14. Returning to the left-hand wing, tie a row of diagonal double half hitch knots with the left-hand set of working cords. Make the right-hand cord of the set your static cord, and working from the centre out to the left-hand edge, tie diagonal double half hitch knots onto it with all of the hanging cords of the left-hand side. No curving this time, just a nice straight diagonal from the centre down to the left.

15. Now working on the right-hand wing, tie a row of diagonal double half hitch knots with the right-hand set of working cords. Make the left-hand cord of the set your static cord, and working from the centre out to the right-hand edge, tie diagonal double half hitch knots onto it with all of the hanging cords of the right-hand side.

16. Now attach the 80cm (32in) fringing cords to the edges of the completed wings, twenty-five to each side. Working between the top of the diagonal double half hitch row and the first row of square knots, attach ten fringing cords using reverse lark's head knots (see Single-Strand Knots), working the knots over two cords at the outer edge. Working between the top of the first row of square knots and the bottom of the third row of the curved double half hitch knots, attach five fringing cords, again using reverse lark's head knots, but this time working the knots over only one cord at the outer edge, and continue in the same way to attach five fringing cords between the third and second rows of the curved double half hitch knots, tying the remaining five fringing cords between the second and first rows (F).

17. Finally, all that remains is to cut the shape into the hanging cords at the base of the hanging. First, identify any fringing lengths as these shouldn't need trimming and will flow nicely when hanging if you have measured accurately. With these out of the way, cut the working cords from the centre to the outer edge at each side, matching the angle of the diagonal double half hitch row above.

TASSELS CHAIN

Give a simple half knot spiral an upgrade to make this sophisticated piece of boho art for your home, featuring rustic wooden bead accents and pretty wrap knot tassels. I've chosen a soft colour palette to create my sweet piece of wall décor, but you can choose shades to suit your preferences. It can easily be adapted, for example, to make a rainbow tassel chain for a child's bedroom.

MATERIALS

- 7m (23ft) of 3-ply 3mm (⅛in) macramé cord (natural)
- 1.8m (6ft) of single-ply 3mm (⅛in) macramé cord in eight different colours
- 8 x large wooden beads
- 2 x 5.5cm (2¼in) wooden rings

FINISHED SIZE

Width (of chain): 110cm (44in)

PREPARATION

- Cut 2 x 3.5m (11½ft) lengths of natural cord
- Cut 2 x 40cm (16in) lengths of each colour cord
- Cut 4 x 25cm (10in) lengths of each colour cord

KNOTS

- Forward Lark's Head Knot
- Square Knot
- Half Knot Spiral

PATTERN NOTES

Following the set up (i.e. attaching the working cords to the starting wooden ring and the addition of the first bead), the central chain is made up of seven sections of half knot spirals. Each of these sections is tied with the same number of knots and ends with the threading on of a bead. At the end of each section, give your knots a twist before moving on to the begin the next section.

Once the central chain is complete, finishing off by attaching the working cords to the second wooden ring, the wrap knot tassels are tied directly onto cords alongside the beads.

You can either hang the starting wooden ring from a clothes rail using an S-hook to work vertically when making this project, or you can secure the wooden ring to your worktop with some tape, as you prefer.

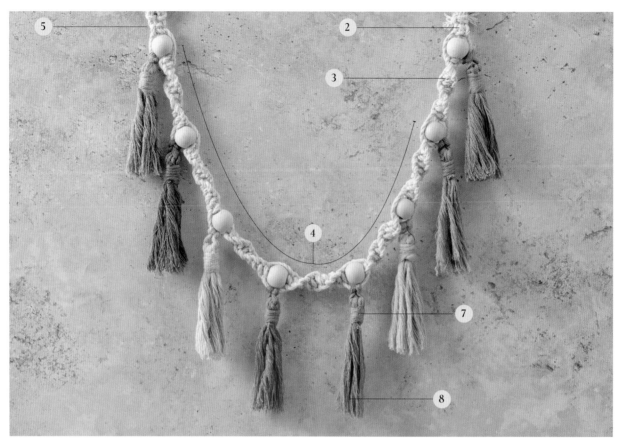

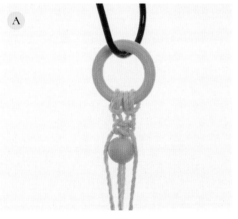

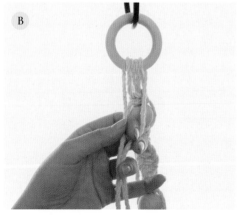

METHOD

1. Take each 3.5m (11½ft) length of cord and fold to measure 2.3m (7½ft) on one side and 1.2m (4ft) on the other. Attach cords to the wooden ring with forward lark's head knots (see Single-Strand Knots), making sure that the longer lengths are on the outside and the shorter lengths are on the inside.

2. Tie a square knot (see Square Knots) tight to the ring. Slide a bead onto the middle two cords, making sure it is placed right up against the square knot (A).

3. Tie the first half knot of your half knot spiral (see Square Knots), to secure the bead's position. Continue to tie the half knot spiral, working a total of ten half knots in all (including the knot that secured the bead's position) to complete the first section of the chain.

4. Take another bead and slide it onto the middle two cords and repeat step 3 to complete the next section of the chain, and continue to work each section of the chain in the same way until you have just completed the final (seventh) half knot spiral section. You should have one bead remaining.

5. Take the final bead and slide it onto the middle two cords as before, then tie a square knot tight to the bead to secure it in place.

6. To attach the second ring to the chain, hang the ring onto an S-hook, and bring the ends of the working cords over the bottom of the second ring from front to back. Identify the outside cords and use them to tie a square knot around all of the hanging cords directly above the last square knot tied (B). Cut the remaining lengths close to the knot.

7. Now you are going to make a wrap knot tassel at the base of each of the accent beads on the chain, eight tassels in all; starting at one end of the chain, take a 40cm (16in) length of the colour cord, fold it in half and attach it to the single loop of cord beneath the first bead using a reverse lark's head knot (see Single-Strand Knots). Bundle together four lengths of 25cm (10in) cord of the same colour and lay them in between the two cords at the base of the lark's head knot (C), tying an overhand knot with these two cords in the middle of the bundle of cords. Tie a second overhand knot to secure the cord bundle in place (D), then fold the cords over the double overhand knot to conceal it. Taking a 40cm (16in) length of same-colour cord, use it to tie a wrap knot (five wraps) at the top of the bundle, just under the concealed double overhand knot. Trim any lengths remaining at the wrap knot to complete the tassel (E). Continue to tie a tassel at the base of each of the beads all the way along the chain.

8. Once all the tassels are complete, use a pet hairbrush to brush out the cord lengths of each of the them and trim as necessary so that all the tassels are the same length.

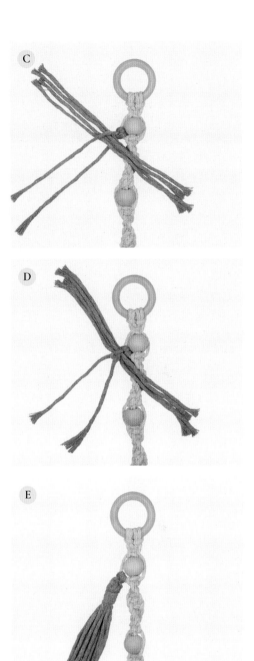

CHRISTMAS DECORATIONS

MATERIALS

Snowflake
- 11.7m (38¼ft) of 3mm (⅛in) macramé cord
- 1 x 5.5cm (2¼in) wooden ring

Wreath
- 2m (6½ft) of 3mm (⅛in) red cord
- 2m (6½ft) of 3mm (⅛in) natural cord
- 1 x 7.5cm (3in) wooden ring

FINISHED SIZE

Snowflake
Width: 13cm (5in)
Length: 13cm (5in)

Wreath
Width: 7.6cm (3¹⁄₁₆in)
Length: 7.6cm (3¹⁄₁₆in)

Transform simple wooden rings into festive décor to bring a unique touch to your Christmas tree with simple macramé techniques. The miniature wreath is created using a half knot spiral and, if you're a beginner, it's a great place to start. Then move on to create the six-pointed snowflake, where you'll be using square knots and diagonal double half hitches to achieve the delicate pattern.

PATTERN NOTES

The six-pointed snowflake is completed one section at a time, repeating around the wooden ring.

For the wreath, the wooden ring itself becomes the foundation onto which the knots are tied. The half knot spiral technique used works most effectively when two contrasting colours are chosen.

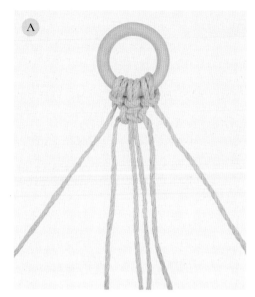

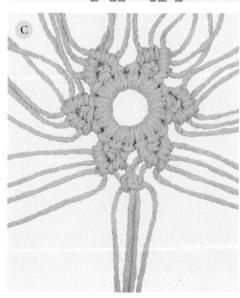

PREPARATION FOR SNOWFLAKE
- Cut 18 x 65cm (25½in) lengths of cord

KNOTS
- Forward Lark's Head Knot
- Square Knot
- Diagonal Double Half Hitches

METHOD FOR SNOWFLAKE

1. Take three 65cm (25½in) lengths of cord, fold each in half and attach to the ring using forward lark's head knots (see Single-Strand Knots), to give you six working cords.

2. Identify the middle four cords (cords 2 to 5) and tie a square knot (see Square Knots) (A), leaving the cords at either side untied.

3. Bring the left-hand (cord 1) down diagonally towards the middle to become a static cord and tie diagonal double half hitches onto it using cords 2 and 3 (see Half Hitch Knots). Mirroring these actions on the right-hand side, bring the right-hand cord (cord 6) down diagonally towards the middle to become a static cord and tie diagonal double half hitches onto it using cords 5 and 4, to create one of the 'points' of your six-pointed snowflake (B).

4. Repeat steps 1 to 3 to create five more 'point' sections, to completely cover the ring.

5. Working between two 'point' sections, join the working cords of one to the other by using two cords from each section to tie a square knot (C). Note that at the point of each arm there should be two hanging cords left unworked.

6. Repeat step 5 all the way around, until all sections of the snowflake are joined (six square knots in total).

7. Choose an arm to be the top of your snowflake and join the two unworked cords at the tail ends with an overhand knot, to make a hanging loop.

8. Trim all other cord ends short to make a little fringe all the way around your finished snowflake.

PREPARATION FOR WREATH

- Cut 1 x 2m (6½ft) length of red cord
- Cut 1 x 2m (6½ft) length of natural cord

KNOTS

- Overhand Knot
- Half Knot Spiral

METHOD FOR WREATH

1. Take two 2m (6½ft) lengths of contrasting cord and join them together at one end using an overhand knot (see Single-Strand Knots). Tape the knotted end to your work surface, so that the white cord is on the left-hand side and the red cord is on the right (A).

2. Holding the ring vertically and starting approximately 10cm (4in) from the taped end, begin to tie a half knot spiral (see Square Knots). Note that when working this technique on the wreath, the working cords are woven over and behind the wooden ring, which takes the place of the static central cords. As you weave the pattern, it is helpful to remember that the cord that is on the left is the cord that rests in front of the wooden ring, while the cord that is on the right is the one that moves over the tail of the left-hand cord and around the back of the ring, to be brought out and over the left-hand cord (B, C). Tie the first two half knots to create a secure wraparound of the wooden ring, then continue to tie half knots all the way around the ring to return to the start point. The spiral will begin to naturally occur as you tie the knots, but it is best to try to stop the twisting effect to stay on track with the order of tying the cords.

3. Once the ring is completely covered, then twist the knots to create the spiral pattern all the way around.

4. When you are happy with the spiral effect, join the ends of the working cords with an overhand knot approximately 10cm (4in) from the ring. This now forms a second hanging loop. Trim the ends of the cords to complete the decoration.

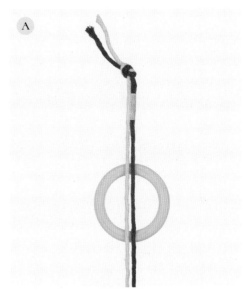

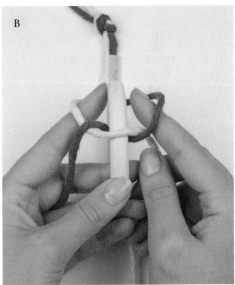

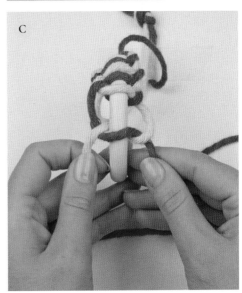

SHOOTING STAR

DIFFICULTY

MATERIALS
- 13.5m (45ft) of 4mm (⁵⁄₃₂in) single-ply macramé cord

FINISHED SIZE
Width: 15cm (6in)
Length: 55cm (21¾in)

PREPARATION
- Cut 15 x 90cm (3ft) lengths of cord

KNOTS
- Reverse Lark's Head Knot
- Square Knot

When it comes to making this shooting star decoration, no wooden ring is required to make its central circular shape. Instead, macramé cord is used as the foundation, which is then joined to make its round centre. Once the foundation ring is formed, simple square knots stacked on top of each other using a weaving technique create the arms and trailing fringe of a 'shooting' star.

PATTERN NOTES

The shooting star pattern is worked in rounds instead of rows, so carefully read through all the instructions first to understand how the cords that form each arm weave into the next.

Work this project on your desktop, and rotate it in the same direction each time when tying the knots on each arm to form the round.

To achieve the shooting star effect, leave the working cords untrimmed at the end to form a long trail, although it can be nice when working with a single-ply cord to brush a little at the bottom of each cord.

METHOD

1. Take one of your 90cm (3ft) lengths of cord, fold it in half and place it horizontally on your work surface, so that the fold is on the left-hand side. This will be the foundation cord. Starting about 1cm (⅜in) from the folded end, attach the remaining fourteen lengths of 90cm (3ft) cord to the foundation cord using reverse lark's head knots (see Single-Strand Knots). Take the ends of the foundation cord and pass them through the loop at the other end of it, pulling the tail ends to form the working cords into a round shape (A). Pull the ends of the foundation cords as tight as possible to minimize the space in the middle of the circle.

2. Orientate your work so that the tail ends of the foundation cord are pointing straight down towards you. Identify the cords to either side of the foundation cord ends, so that you now have four cords, and tie a square knot (see Square Knots).

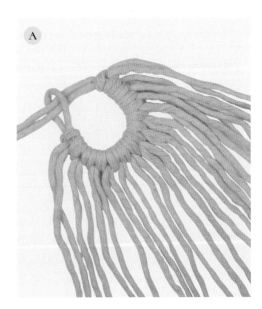

A

3. Leaving the two hanging cords to the left of the square knot unworked, identify the next four hanging cords and tie another square knot (B). Repeat this pattern to tie your first round of square knots (five in total). Once the round is complete, there will be two hanging cords left unworked at either side of the square knots.

4. For the second round, choose one of the square knots from the first round and identify a single hanging cord to either side of it so that you have six cords in front of you. Take cords 1 and 6 over cords 2 and 5 (i.e. the previous working cords), and tie a square knot over the static cords (i.e. cords 3 and 4) (C). Repeat this process all the way around to complete the second round; another five square knots have been tied and the arms of your star have grown a little longer. Once the round is complete, each arm of the star has six cords with one hanging cord left unworked to either side of it.

5. In the third and final round of square knots, the points of the star will be formed. Choose one of the square knots from the second round and take the unworked hanging cord at either side of it over the working cords from the previous round, to tie a square knot over the central static cords (D). Repeat this process all the way around to complete the final round; another five square knots have been tied and the arms of your star have now been formed into points.

6. Choose which of the arms you want to be at the top of the star, and make a hanging loop by tying an overhand knot (see Single-Strand Knots) with the static cords in the middle. Trim off the excess cords at the end of the overhand knot.

7. Hang the star and give its fringes a brush out to loosen their twist a little (not all the way), using a pet hairbrush. Personally, I like to leave the hanging cords untrimmed as I think it adds to the aesthetic, but you can use a pair of scissors to level off the bottom if you see fit.

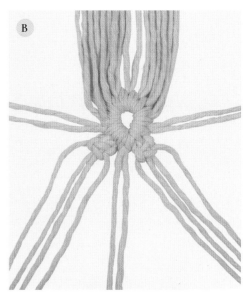

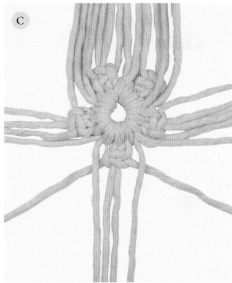

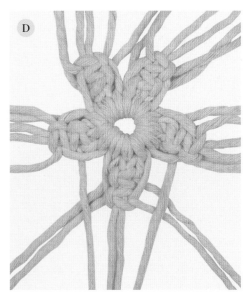

SQUARE KNOT WALL HANGING

MATERIALS
- 27.6m (91ft) of 5mm (³⁄₁₆in) 3-ply macramé cord
- 25cm (10in) length of 20mm (¾in) wooden dowel

FINISHED SIZE
Width: 21cm (8¼in)

Length: 48cm (19in)

PREPARATION
- Cut 10 x 1.4m (55in) lengths of cord
- Cut 6 x 1.3m (51¼in) lengths of cord
- Cut 7 x 60cm (24in) lengths of cord
- Cut 2 x 80cm (32in) lengths of cord

KNOTS
- Forward Lark's Head Knot
- Six-Strand Braid
- Wrap Knot

If you are a beginner looking for a first wall hanging project, this little panel is a brilliant project to get you started. Inspired by the wall hangings of the 1970s, it'll extend your repertoire of creating triangles using the alternating square knot pattern, while giving you a chance to practise six-strand braids and wrap knots for the tassel fringing. It has a lovely chunky rope finish and is quick to make.

PATTERN NOTES

The pattern is worked in two stages: first, working cords are attached for the tying of the alternating square knot triangle design of the central panel; second, additional working cords are attached for working the six-strand braids to either side of the central panel.

To make the central panel design, rows of alternating square knots are worked to create a sequence of alternating square knot triangles. Before beginning this project, you may find it helpful to review the Triangles and Diamonds Chain (see Six-Cord Chains).

It is recommended that you hang the dowel from a clothes rail using S-hooks to work vertically when making this project.

METHOD

Central Panel

1. Take the ten 1.4m (55in) lengths of cord, fold each in half and attach them in the centre of the dowel using forward lark's head knot (see Single-Strand Knots), to give you twenty working cords.

2. Work the small, downward-pointing triangle using an alternating square knot pattern, as follows:

Row 1: Tie a square knot with the central cords (cords 9 to 12), then tie a square knot to either side using cords 5 to 8 and cords 13 to 16 (three square knots in total). Note: there will be two hanging cords at each edge untied.

Row 2: Alternating cords with the row above, tie a row of two square knots using cords 7 to 10 and 11 to 14.

Row 3: Alternating cords with the row above, tie one square knot using cords 9 to 12.

3. Work the large downward-pointing triangle using an alternating square knot pattern, as follows:

Row 4: Tie a row of square knots across all working cords (five square knots in total).

Row 5: Alternating cords with the row above, tie a row of four square knots using cords 3 to 6, 7 to 10, 11 to 14, 15 to 18.

Row 6: Alternating cords with the row above, tie a row of three square knots using cords 5 to 8, 9 to 12, 13 to 16.

Row 7: Alternating cords with the row above, tie a row of two square knots using cords 7 to 10 and 11 to 14.

Row 8: Alternating cords with the row above, tie one square knot using cords 9 to 12.

4. Work the small upward-pointing triangle using an alternating square knot pattern, as follows:

Row 9: Tie one square knot using cords 9 to 12.

Row 10: Alternating cords with the row above, tie a row of two square knots using cords 7 to 10 and 11 to 14.

Row 11: Alternating cords with the row above, tie a row of three square knots using cords 5 to 8, 9 to 12, 13 to 16.

5. Work the large upward-pointing triangle using an alternating square knot pattern, as follows:

Row 12: Repeat Row 9.

Row 13: Repeat Row 10.

Row 14: Repeat Row 11.

Row 15: Alternating cords with the row above, tie a row of four square knots using cords 3 to 6, 7 to 10, 11 to 14, 15 to 18.

Row 16: Tie a row of square knots across all working cords (five square knots in total).

Six-Strand Braids

6. Take three 1.3m (51¼in) lengths of cord, fold each in half and attach them to the dowel to the left-hand side of the completed central panel using forward lark's head knots, to give you six working cords.

7. Tie a six-strand braid (see Braids) that reaches to the last row of square knots in the central panel.

8. Take a 40cm (16in) length of cord and tie a wrap knot (five wraps) around the working cords at the bottom of the braid (see Single-Strand Knots).

9. Take three 1.3m (51¼in) lengths of cord, fold each in half and attach them to the dowel to the right-hand side of the completed central panel using forward lark's head knot, to give you six working cords.

10. Repeat steps 7 and 8 to complete the right-hand six-strand braid.

Finishing

11. Finish off the bottom of the hanging by adding a wrap knot below each square knot on the last row of the central panel (five in all). Using a 60cm (24in) length of cord, tie each with five wraps.

12. Trim all cord lengths beneath the wrap knots to be the same length.

13. Taking the remaining two 80cm (32in) lengths of cords, create a hanging loop for your wall hanging (see Finishing Methods).

LEOPARD PRINT WALL HANGING

DIFFICULTY

This pixel art wall hanging requires a sound knowledge of the vertical double half hitch. You'll be switching cord colours as you work, following a pattern chart to guide you, and the beautiful animal print begins to be revealed as you complete row after row. The finished piece is a woven-style masterpiece that brings a bit of sass to the home.

MATERIALS

- 36.4m (118ft) of 3mm (⅛in) single-ply macramé cord in background colour (beige)
- 500m (547yd) roll of 3mm (⅛in) single-ply macramé cord in two additional colours (brown and mustard)
- 35cm (13¾in) length of 22mm (⅞in) wooden dowel

FINISHED SIZE

Width: 28cm (11in)
Length: 110cm (44in)

PREPARATION

- Cut 28 x 1.2m (4ft) lengths of background colour cord (beige)
- Cut 2 x 40cm (16in) lengths of background colour cord (beige)
- Cut 2 x 1m (3¼ft) lengths of background colour cord (beige)

KNOTS

- Reverse Lark's Head Knot
- Horizontal Double Half Hitches
- Vertical Double Half Hitches

PATTERN NOTES

It is recommended that you hang the dowel from a clothes rail using S-hooks to work vertically when making this project; you'll need a clip or peg to help secure cords at the side when adding in new lengths of colour.

A single row of horizontal double half hitch borders the leopard print design and this is not charted. For the leopard print design, refer to the chart for cord colour changes. Each square represents a vertical double half hitch worked over a pair of static hanging cords. Work odd numbered rows from left to right; work even numbered rows from right to left.

It is recommended that you measure and cut 5m (16½ft) lengths of the cord lengths for the cord colour changes as they are required. Be sure to have a good supply of each of your chosen colours; I recommend at least a 500m (547yd) roll of each.

The back of this hanging will be tidied up at the end so don't worry about how it looks, just focus on tying your knots consistently on the front.

METHOD

1. Take the twenty-eight 1.2m (4ft) lengths of cord, fold each in half and attach them to the dowel using reverse lark's head knot (see Single-Strand Knots), to give you fifty-six hanging cords.

2. Take a 40cm (16in) length of cord and attach one end to the clip at the left-hand side of your clothes rail. Bringing it horizontally across the hanging cords to be your static cord, tie a horizontal double half hitch knot (see Half Hitch Knots) with each of the hanging cords onto it.

3. You are now ready to begin the leopard print design. Now each pair of hanging cords becomes the static cords over which you will work vertical double half hitches, using the colour cords identified in the leopard print chart (see Half Hitch Knots: Colour Changes Using Vertical Double Half Hitch). Let's look in detail at the working of Row 1, as follows:

   Row 1, Beige 1 & 2: Measure and cut a 5m (16½ft) length of beige cord and attach one end to the clip at the left-hand side of your clothes rail. Taking the working length of the cord behind the first pair of hanging cords, use it to tie a vertical double half hitch (see Half Hitch Knots) onto these hanging cords. Then continue to use the beige working cord to tie a second vertical double half hitch around the next pair of hanging cords. Leave the beige working cord hanging behind the project ready to be picked up again later in the row.

   Row 1, Brown 3 to 6: Measure and cut a 5m (16½ft) length of brown cord and attach one end to the clip at the left-hand side of your clothes rail. Taking the working length of the cord behind the first two pairs of hanging cords, use it to tie four vertical double half hitches onto the next four pairs of hanging cords (A). Leave the brown working cord hanging behind the project ready to be picked up again later in the row.

Row 1, Beige 7 to 10: Identify the working length of beige cord left hanging earlier in the row, pull it gently behind the brown knots and use it to tie four vertical double half hitches onto the next four pairs of hanging cords. Again, leave the beige working cord hanging behind the project ready to be picked up again later in the row.

Row 1, Brown 11 & 12: Identify the working length of brown cord left hanging earlier in the row, pull it gently behind the beige knots and use it to tie two vertical double half hitches onto the next two pairs of hanging cords. Again, leave the brown working cord hanging behind the project ready to be picked up again later in the row.

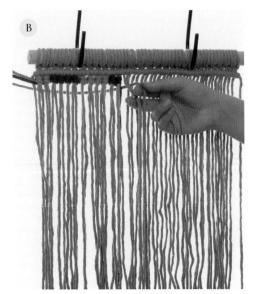

Row 1, Mustard 13: Measure and cut a 5m (16½ft) length of mustard cord and attach one end to the clip at the left-hand side of your clothes rail. Taking the working length of the cord behind the stitches already worked, use it to tie one vertical double half hitch onto the next pair of hanging cords (B). Leave the mustard working cord hanging behind the project ready to be picked up again later towards the end of the row.

Row 1, Brown 14 & 15: Identify the working length of the brown cord and bring it across the back of the project to use it to tie two vertical double half hitches onto the next two pairs of hanging cords, then leave it hanging.

Row 1, Beige 16 to 22: Identify the working length of the beige cord and bring it across the back of the project to use it to tie six vertical double half hitches onto the next six pairs of hanging cords, then leave it hanging.

Row 1, Brown 23 & 24: Identify the working length of the brown cord and bring it across the back of the project to use it to tie two vertical double half hitches onto the next two pairs of hanging cords, then leave it hanging.

Row 1, Mustard 25 to 28: Identify the working length of the mustard cord and bring it across the back of the project to use it to tie four vertical double half hitches onto the next four pairs of hanging cords, then leave it hanging.

This completes the first row of the chart of the leopard print design (C).

4. For Row 2, continue to follow the chart, switching between the working lengths of colour cord as required, this time working from right to left across the row to minimize the amount of cord that needs to be carried over the back of the project between stitches.

5. Carefully following the chart, continue to work the remaining rows, Rows 3 to 20, working from left to right for odd numbered rows and right to left for even numbered rows. When you run out of a length of working cord, simply leave the tail behind the project and add in another length from the clip on the left-hand side of your clothes rail. Vertical double half hitches are secure by themselves so there is no need to worry about the project unravelling.

6. To complete the tying of the wall hanging, repeat step 2 to work a row of horizontal double half hitches onto the remaining length of 40cm (16in) cord.

7. Cut the hanging cords to your preferred length and brush out into a fringe as you prefer. The back of your hanging will be a mass of carried-over lengths and these can be cut and trimmed if you choose to do so. Personally, I like to cover them with a rectangle of self-adhesive felt.

8. Taking the two 1m (3¼ft) lengths of background colour cords, create a hanging loop for your wall hanging (see Finishing Methods).

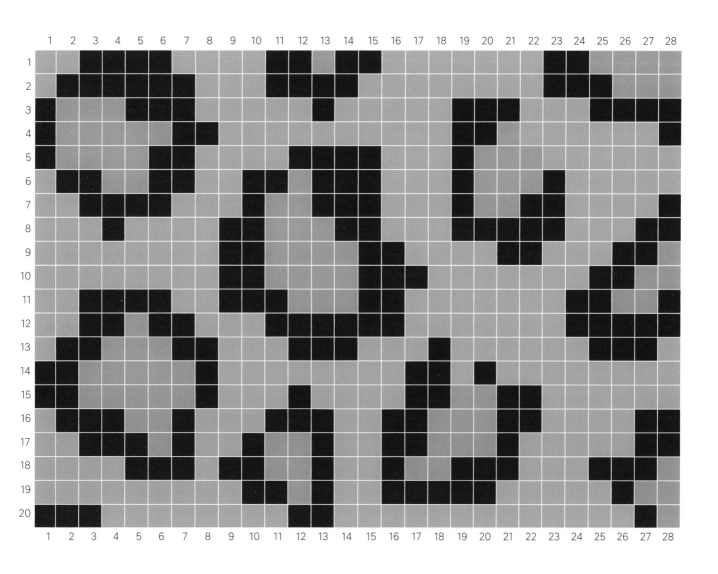

BEGINNER'S TALISMAN

DIFFICULTY

MATERIALS
- 50.8m (163½ft) of 4mm (⁵⁄₃₂in) 3-ply macramé cord
- 30cm (12in) length of 20mm (¾in) wooden dowel

FINISHED SIZE
Width: 29cm (11⅜in)
Length: 50cm (20in)

PREPARATION
- Cut 18 x 1.3m (51¼in) lengths of cord
- Cut 2 x 1.5m (5ft) lengths of cord
- Cut 32 x 70cm (27½in) lengths of cord
- Cut 2 x 1m (3¼ft) lengths of cord

KNOTS
- Forward Lark's Head Knot
- Square Knot
- Alternating Square Knots
- Diagonal Double Half Hitches

If you are new to the world of talisman wall hangings, then this is the project for you as it is made using just two layers. The design on the back layer revisits diamond motifs made with diagonal half hitch knots and alternating square knots, first seen in the Six-Cord Chains chapter, and it's framed with a top layer of softly shaped fringing. It's a quick way to achieve that boho vibe.

PATTERN NOTES

It is recommended that you hang the dowel from a clothes rail using S-hooks to work vertically when making this project.

Refer to Six-Cord Chains for illustrated steps for making a diagonal double half hitch diamond with alternating square knot centre.

METHOD

1. Take the eighteen 1.3m (51¼in) lengths of cord, fold them in half and attach to the dowel using forward lark's head knots (see Single-Strand Knots), to give you thirty-six working cords.

2. Separate out the cords into three sections with twelve hanging cords in each section. Working on the centre section of twelve working cords, find the middle two cords and join with a half knot (see Square Knots). These cords will become the static cords that the diagonal double half hitches will be tied onto to form the top of the diamond motif.

3. Working from the centre to the left, place the left-hand static cord diagonally and tie five diagonal double half hitches onto it with the left-hand hanging cords (see Half Hitch Knots) .

4. Then, mirroring your actions on the right-hand side, take the right-hand static cord and tie five diagonal double half hitches onto it with the right-hand hanging cords (A).

5. Identity the middle four cords and tie a square knot (see Square Knots).

6. Directly below, separate the working cords of the square knot to identify the two left-hand cords. Taking these together with the two hanging cords to the left, tie the first of two square knots on this row. Identifying the two right-hand cords from the square knot above and taking these together with the two hanging cords to the right, tie the second square knot in an alternating square knot pattern.

7. Directly below, identify the middle four cords once more and tie a square knot to complete the alternating square knot pattern.

8. To form the bottom of the diamond motif, take the far left-hand cord and place it diagonally into the centre. This becomes the static cord onto which five diagonal double half hitches will be tied with the hanging cords, working from the left to the middle. Mirror your actions on the right-hand side, bringing the far right-hand cord diagonally into the centre, working from the right to the middle tying five diagonal double half hitches. Join the static cords in the middle using a half knot.

9. Directly below the diagonal double half hitch diamond, repeat steps 5 to 7 to tie a small diamond using alternating square knots.

10. Now working on the left-hand section of twelve working cords, tie a large diamond using alternating square knots. Start by identifying the middle four cords (cords 5 to 8) and tie a square knot to complete row 1.

11. On row 2, tie two square knots using cords 3 to 6 and cords 7 to 10.

12. On row 3, tie three square knots using cords 1 to 4, cords 5 to 8 and cords 9 to 12.

13. On row 4, tie two square knots using cords 3 to 6 and cords 7 to 10.

14. On row 5, tie one square knot using cords 5 to 8 to complete the diamond motif.

15. Repeat steps 10 to 14 on the right-hand section of twelve working cords to complete the tying of the macramé panel.

16. Take the two 1.5m (5ft) lengths of cord, fold them in half and attach one to either side of the macramé panel using forward lark's head knots, to give you an additional two hanging cords to each side. Join these four cords together with a square knot, so that the knot rests in the same position as the final knot at the base of the large alternating square knot diamond in the middle section of your panel (B). This creates a fringe line that the fringe lengths will be attached to.

17. Attach sixteen of the 70cm (27½in) lengths of cord to each side of the square knot on the fringe line using forward lark's head knot.

18. Taking the two 1m (3¼ft) lengths of cord, create a hanging loop for your wall hanging (C) (see Finishing Methods).

19. Trim the fringe so that all the cord lengths are the same length to complete the hanging.

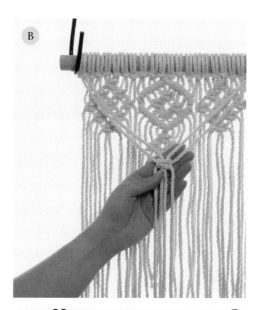

FISHTAIL CHAINS TALISMAN

DIFFICULTY

MATERIALS
- 86.4m (283¼ft) of 6-8mm (¼-⁵⁄₁₆in) single-ply macramé cord
- 60cm (24in) length of 20mm (¾in) wooden dowel

FINISHED SIZE
Width: 50cm (20in)
Length: 90cm (36in)

PREPARATION
- Cut 4 x 4.7m (15½ft) lengths of cord
- Cut 1 x 2.8m (9¼ft) length of cord
- Cut 24 x 2m (6½ft) lengths of cord
- Cut 36 x 40cm (16in) lengths of cord
- Cut 2 x 1.2m (4ft) lengths of cord

KNOTS
- Overhand Knot
- Forward Lark's Head Knot
- Reverse Lark's Head Knot
- Diagonal Double Half Hitches
- Square Knot
- Alternating Square Knots

This talisman wall hanging creates quite an impact with its use of a chunky single-ply cord. It's created in two layers, with a top layer that makes the most of its fishtail diamond chains, framing them with beautifully brushed out fringing. The top layer chains are joined with an alternating square knot pattern that is repeated on the back layer panel too, which transitions into even more fringing, making this a real show-stopper.

PATTERN NOTES

Choosing a single-ply cord is essential for this project if you want to achieve the beautiful, brushed out fringing seen here. The chunkier the cord you choose the better, so you can go up to an 8mm (⁵⁄₁₆in) cord if you wish.

It is recommended that you hang the dowel from a clothes rail using S-hooks to work vertically when making this project.

Refer to Four-Cord Chains for illustrated steps for making a fishtail chain.

METHOD

Top Layer

1. Take two 4.7m (15½ft) lengths of cord, fold each in half and attach them to one end of the dowel using forward lark's head knots (see Single-Strand Knots), to give you eight working cords.

2. Referring to Four-Cord Chains: Fishtail Chain, tie a chain of five diagonal double half hitch diamonds in the fishtail style.

3. Repeat steps 1 and 2 to make a second fishtail chain using the remaining two lengths of 4.7m (15½ft) cord, working close to the other end of the dowel.

4. Once the chains are complete, they need to be joined with a square knot. First identify the four cords to be used; these are the two hanging cords that are at the inside edge of each of the diamonds at the bottom of each chain. Use these four cords to tie a square knot, pulling them tightly to bring the chains together (A).

5. Directly below, tie the middle cords of the square knot together with a half knot and create a diagonal double half hitch diamond exactly as before (B).

6. Use the hanging cords from this diagonal double half hitch diamond to tie two square knots, one to each side (C).

7. Then using the four cords left hanging at each side, tie two more square knots, one to each side (D). This completes the first row of square knots (four in total).

8. Alternating cords, tie a second row of three square knots (E).

9. Leaving a space of approx. 6cm (2⅜in), tie a row of two alternating square knots.

10. Leaving a space of approx. 6cm (2⅜in), tie one square knot using the four middle cords.

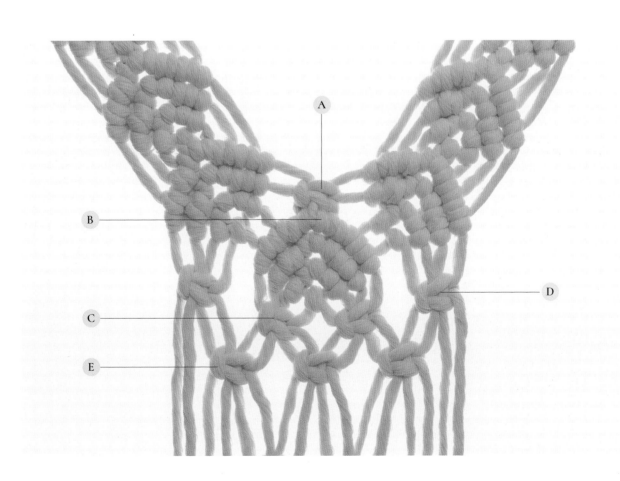

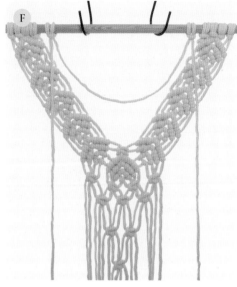

Back Layer

11. Take the 2.8m (9¼ft) length of cord and folding it approx. 80cm (32in) from the end, attach it to the dowel on the inside edge of the left-hand chain, using a forward lark's head knot. Use the looping lark's head technique (see Getting Started) to attach the other end of the cord to the dowel on the inside edge of the right-hand chain, leaving an end of approx. 80cm (32in). Adjust the cords so that there is an 80cm (32in) length at either side and a deep U-shape between the two (F). This outlines the back layer fringe line. Take the twenty-four lengths of 2m (6½ft) cord, fold each in half and attach them across the fringe line using forward lark's head knots, to give you forty-eight working cords.

12. Identify the 80cm (32in) length of cord at the left-hand edge of the fringe line and bring it diagonally towards the middle (G). This becomes the static cord onto which you will tie diagonal double half hitches with the left-hand set of twenty-four hanging cords, working from the left to the middle.

13. Mirroring your actions on the right-hand side, identify the 80cm (32in) length of cord at the right-hand edge of the fringe line and bring it diagonally towards the middle (H). This becomes the static cord onto which you will tie diagonal double half hitches with the right-hand set of twenty-four hanging cords, working from the right to the middle.

14. Starting from the outside and working inwards on both sides, tie a row of twelve square knots (six at either side with two hanging cords untied in the middle) (I).

15. Starting in the middle and alternating cords with the square knots in the row above, tie a row of seven square knots.

16. Starting in the middle and alternating cords with the square knots in the row above, tie a third and final row of four square knots to complete the fringed back layer.

Finishing

17. Place the back layer behind the top (chains) layer in preparation to add the fringing lengths to the outside cords of the chains. Starting from the top, in the space between the dowel and top of the first fishtail diamond, attach two 40cm (16in) lengths of cord using reverse lark's head knots. Then, alongside each of the first four fishtail diamonds on either side, attach four 40cm (16in) lengths of cord using reverse lark's head knots. Use a pet hairbrush to brush out the fringe lengths added. Trim the fringe into graduated steps on each side.

18. Brush the fringing on the back layer of the talisman to fluff it up a bit.

19. Taking the two 1.2m (4ft) lengths of cord, create a hanging loop for your wall hanging (see Finishing Methods), positioning the cords on the dowel in the space between the two layers.

TRIPLE LAYER
TALISMAN

DIFFICULTY

MATERIALS

- 100m (332½ft) of 4mm (⁵⁄₃₂in) 3-ply macramé cord
- 38cm (15in) length of 20mm (¾in) wooden dowel

FINISHED SIZE

Width: 35cm (13¾in)
Length: 57cm (22½in)

If you are looking for a challenge, then this wall hanging is the project for you. It has three layers: the main panel, which is the back layer, features patterns you were introduced to in Four-Cord Chains, while the top layer is made from two joined diamond chains, and in between the two is a spectacular fringing layer created with two lengths of fringe. Decorative tassels complete the look.

PATTERN NOTES

It is recommended that you hang the dowel from a clothes rail using S-hooks to work vertically when making this project.

One of the most complex parts of this project is the management of so many cord lengths, so you might want to cut and measure the cords required for each layer as you come to tie them.

Follow the steps carefully and you will discover that this many layered project is actually quite simple to make.

PREPARATION

Main Panel
- Cut 14 x 1.8m (6ft) lengths of cord

Chain Layer
- Cut 6 x 3m (10ft) lengths of cord

Fringe Line 1
- Cut 1 x 2.7m (9ft) length of cord

Fringe Lengths for Fringe 1
- Cut 40 x 80cm (32in) lengths of cord

Fringe Lengths for Fringe 2
- Cut 14 x 55cm (21¾in) lengths of cord

Per Tassel (12 in total)
- Cut 4 x 25cm (10in) lengths of cord
- Cut 1 x 40cm (16in) length of cord

Hanging Loop
- Cut 2 x 90cm (3ft) lengths of cord

KNOTS
- Overhand Knot
- Forward Lark's Head Knot
- Diagonal Double Half Hitches
- Square Knot
- Alternating Square Knots

MAIN PANEL

FRINGE LINE 1

FRINGE LINE 2

METHOD

Main Panel

1. Take fourteen 1.8m (6ft) lengths of cord, fold each in half and attach to the dowel using forward lark's head knots (see Single-Strand Knots), to give you fourteen pairs of hanging cords. Separate into three groups: four pairs to the left, six in the middle and four to the right. Referring to photo (A) for detail view, tie main panel design as described in the following steps.

2. Working with the first four pairs of hanging cords, create a diagonal double half hitch diamond with square knot centre (see Four-Cord Chains: Diagonal DHH Diamond Chain with Square Knots, steps 2 to 5). Repeat with the last four pairs of hanging cords.

3. Working with the six pairs of hanging cords in the middle, tie two square knots (see Square Knots) next to each other, leaving a pair of hanging cords at either side.

4. Directly below, tie an alternating square knot to each side working diagonally outwards.

5. Repeat step 4. Note that the square knots on this row now join the middle group of cords with those to either side.

6. Repeat step 5 to complete your square knot diagonals from the middle out (four square knots to each side).

7. Create the large diamond in the middle of the main panel following the line established by the diagonal rows of diagonal square knots to either side. The method is the same as steps 2 to 10 for working the diamond motif in the diagonal double half hitch diamond chain with alternating square knot centre (see Six-Cord Chains), except here the static cords are secured with seven diagonal double half hitches to either side at the top and bottom of the diamond motif. When working the final row of diagonal double half hitches at the base of the diamond, secure the static cords with a double half hitch. The main panel is now complete and this will always be at the back of the hanging (A).

Chain Layer

8. Take three 3m (10ft) lengths of cord, fold each in half and attach to the dowel to the left-hand side of the completed main panel, to give you a set of six working cords. To create the first diamond in the chain, join the middle cords with a half knot and, taking the left-hand cord as the static cord, tie two diagonal double half hitches with the left-hand working cords from the centre to the left. Returning to the middle, take the right-hand static cord and tie two diagonal double half hitches with the left-hand working cords from the centre to the right, to complete the top half of the diamond shape.

9. Identifying the middle four cords, tie a square knot.

10. Complete the bottom half of the diamond shape. First take the left-hand static cord and turn it inwards diagonally, tying two diagonal double half hitches with the left-hand working cords in towards the middle. Then take the right-hand static cord and turn it inwards diagonally, tying two diagonal double half hitches with the right-hand working cords in towards the middle.

11. Where the static cords meet in the middle, join them together with a half knot to form the top knot of the next diamond.

12. Tie three more diagonal double half hitch diamonds with square knot centres to complete the chain (four diamonds in total).

13. Repeat steps 8 to 12 to create another chain of four diagonal double half hitch diamonds with square knot centres to the right-hand side of the completed main panel (B).

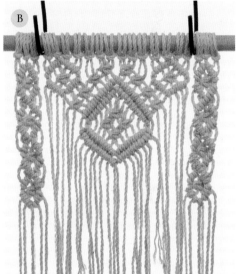

CHAIN LAYER

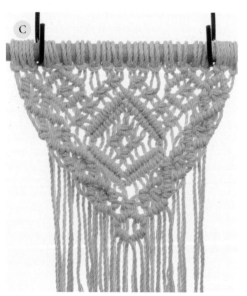

C

14. Once the chains are complete, they need to be joined with a square knot. First identify the four cords to be used; these are the two hanging cords that are at the inside edge of each of the diamonds at the bottom of each chain. Use these four cords to tie a square knot, pulling them tightly to bring the chains together. The square knot join should hang just below the bottom of the main panel diamond.

15. Directly below, tie the middle cords of the square knot together with a half knot and create an 'empty' diagonal double half hitch diamond, made two diagonal double half hitches wide on each diagonal (C).

Fringes

16. Take the 2.7m (9ft) length of cord and folding it approx. 1.2m (4ft) from the end, attach it to the dowel on the left-hand side of the hanging, using a forward lark's head knot. Use the looping lark's head technique (see Getting Started) to attach the other end of the cord to the dowel on the left-hand side of the hanging, leaving an end of approx. 1.2m (4ft). Adjust the cords so that there is a 1.2m (4ft) length at either side and a wide U-shape between the two that is shallower than the joined diamond chains at the base. This outlines fringe line 1, which will be the main fringe on this project.

17. Take the 1.2m (4ft) lengths of cord left hanging at either side of the U-shape and join them with a loose overhand knot to make a second U-shape to match the first. This outlines fringe line 2. Do not tie the knot tight as you may need to manipulate the fringe line shape after the fringe lengths have been added (D). Pull this up and out of the way for the time being.

18. Take the forty lengths of 80cm (32in) cord, fold each in half and attach them evenly across fringe line 1, using forward lark's head knots, to create a full fringe.

19. Bring fringe line 2 back down. If fringe line 1 is hanging below the diamonds on the chains, you will need to make an adjustment prior to adding the fringing lengths to fringe line 2. Untie the overhand knot and pull the lengths to make fringe line 1 tighter, lifting the fringing a little. Once you are happy with the adjustment, re-tie the overhand knot ensuring that it will not be visible when the chain layer is laid over the top.

20. Take the fourteen lengths of 55cm (21¾in) cord, fold each in half and attach them to fringe line 2, seven to either side of the overhand knot, using forward lark's head knots, to create a half fringe.

Finishing

21. Rearrange the different layers of the wall hanging so that the chain layer is on top, the fringe layers beneath with the narrower, shorter fringe (fringe 2) lying on top of the full fringe (fringe 1), and the main panel layer at the back.

22. Trim the hanging lengths beneath the diamond chains to be part of the shorter fringe, cutting them at an angle to make them blend in. You are aiming for a curved effect ending in a point.

23. Now to add the tassels. These are simply made using a bundle of cords placed over a loop of previously worked cord, and these are then fastened with a wrap knot. Start by adding a tassel to the large diamond on the main panel. Slide up the top square knot within the diamond to create a space for the tassel. Identify the middle two cords beneath the square knot and take a bundle of four 25cm (10in) lengths of cord and weave the ends behind these cords, bringing them back out to the front to rest in an upside-down U-shape. Taking a 50cm (20in) length of cord, use it to tie a wrap knot (four wraps) at the top of the bundle.

24. Repeat the tassel-making method described in step 23 to add a tassel to the outer cords at the bottom of the chain layer, five to each side.

25. Again, making the tassel as before, add one final tassel to the middle two cords of the 'empty' diamond that joins the left and right chains. Trim the bottom of the tassels, making sure all are the same length.

26. Taking the two 90cm (3ft) lengths of cord, create a hanging loop for your wall hanging (see Finishing Methods), positioning the cords at the ends of the dowel.

TEMPLATE

This template is shown at actual size. A printable version can be downloaded from www.davidandcharles.com.

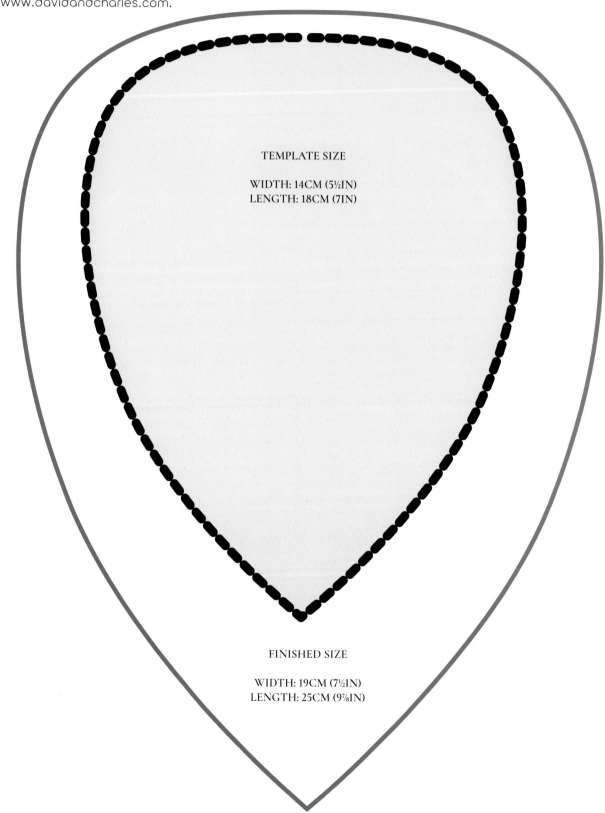

TEMPLATE SIZE

WIDTH: 14CM (5½IN)
LENGTH: 18CM (7IN)

FINISHED SIZE

WIDTH: 19CM (7½IN)
LENGTH: 25CM (9⅞IN)

ABOUT THE AUTHOR

Robyn Gough is a creative designer from Bournemouth, United Kingdom. Robyn has been teaching macramé online via her website and blog at macrameuk.com, and on YouTube and in person for many years. A proud independent business owner and crafter, she has been seen on the BBC television series 'Junk Rescue' and she writes how-to macramé articles, full macramé patterns, and supplies macramé cord and accessories via her online store. Robyn works from a creative studio and offers graphic design, web design, photography and marketing consultancy services. When not being creative, she enjoys long dog walks on the beach with her partner, in the sunny coastal town that she loves to call home.

THANKS

No woman is an island and this book would not be complete without thinking about the journey that got me here and acknowledging the love and support I have received.

I am incredibly lucky to have my parents, my mom and my dad, and the rest of my family, who believed in me finding my way to pursue a creative education and career – their constant support means the world to me, impossible to put into a single paragraph.

I owe a world of gratitude to my love and partner. It has been clear throughout this process that he never thought I would not achieve the end result. A generous and supportive man, he worked extra evenings and weekends alongside his gang of traders and 'merry men' to renovate our home office. This selflessness has given me the creative studio of my dreams to do this work. Without their love and labour, this book would not have been possible.

Special mention is due, too, to another stand-out cheerleader, my friend Siobhan. Always there, always working in the background to support my business and Number 2 at macrameuk.com. When the going gets tough, the tough call in Siobhan! Thank you for believing in my often crazy and lofty ambitions!

My greatest influences of all are my female friends, comrades and colleagues. As well as the women in my direct family, my mothers-in-law, all of my hardworking female friends, female colleagues and my female boss, all have egged me on. Thank you.

Thank you to the creative geniuses at David and Charles and my editor Cheryl. Words are not my strong suit, but you trusted that the macramé would speak for itself and would work tirelessly to prop up the skills I don't possess to make this lovely book happen, which has been inspiring. Thanks for letting my artwork fly.

SUPPLIERS

When seeking macramé materials the best place to look is online. Over recent years there has been a growth in the craft and in the availability of good-quality cotton, but it is still hard to find suitable specialist cords in stores. Macramé cord is either available from manufacturers and factories producing the materials, or independent makers, like myself, who have a cord supply arm to their business. Personally, I believe that buying from a well-established maker is a great way to support your local economy and fellow creatives, and I've offered a few recommendations here. Wherever you choose to shop, it is commonplace to have colour samples supplied, so do not be afraid to ask.

UNITED KINGDOM AND EUROPE

United Knots

www.macrameuk.com

Founded by the author, Robyn Gough

UNITED STATES

Niroma Studio

www.niromastudio.com

Founded by Cindy Hwang Boska

AUSTRALIA

Mary Maker Studio

www.marymakerstudio.com.au

Founded by Brydie Stewart

INDEX

A DAVID AND CHARLES BOOK
© David and Charles, Ltd 2023

David and Charles is an imprint of David and Charles, Ltd
Suite A, Tourism House, Pynes Hill, Exeter, EX2 5WS

Text and Designs © Robyn Gough 2023
Layout and Photography © David and Charles, Ltd 2023

First published in the UK and USA in 2023

Robyn Gough has asserted her right to be identified as
author of this work in accordance with the Copyright,
Designs and Patents Act, 1988.

A catalogue record for this book is available from the
British Library.

ISBN-13: 9781446309728 paperback
ISBN-13: 9781446382387 EPUB

This book has been printed on paper from approved
suppliers and made from pulp from sustainable sources.

FSC
www.fsc.org

MIX
Paper from
responsible sources
FSC® C012521

Printed in China through Asia Pacific Offset for:
David and Charles, Ltd
Suite A, Tourism House, Pynes Hill, Exeter, EX2 5WS

10 9 8 7 6 5 4 3 2

Publishing Director: Ame Verso
Senior Commissioning Editor: Sarah Callard
Managing Editor: Jeni Chown
Project Editor: Cheryl Brown
Head of Design: Anna Wade
Designer: Lucy Ridley and Jo Langdon
Pre-press Designer: Susan Reansbury
Illustrations: Kuo Kang Chen
Art Direction: Sarah Rowntree
Photography: Jason Jenkins
Production Manager: Beverley Richardson

David and Charles publishes high-quality books on
a wide range of subjects. For more information visit
www.davidandcharles.com.

Share your makes with us on social media using
#dandcbooks and follow us on Facebook and Instagram
by searching for @dandcbooks.

Layout of the digital edition of this book may vary
depending on reader hardware and display settings.